MULTIPLYING
MISSIONAL LEADERS

From half-hearted volunteers to a mobilized Kingdom force

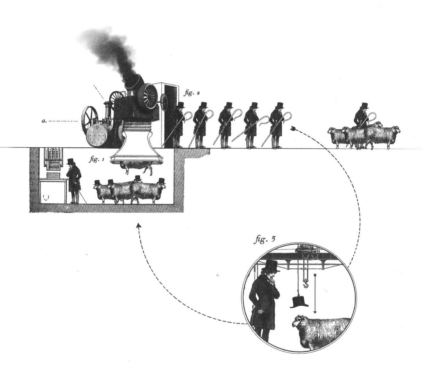

Mike Breen

First printing 2012
Printed in China
4 5 6 7 8 9 10 11 12 13 Printing/Year 15 14 13 12 11 10

Cover Design: Blake Berg
Editor/Interior Design: Pete Berg
ISBN: 978-0-9846643-1-3

This book is dedicated to everyone part of The Order of Mission. This is the story of how you live your life each and every day.

ACKNOWLEDGEMENTS

A special thanks to the Content Team at 3DM: Doug Paul, the Director of Content, for tirelessly working through the ideas, manuscripts and continual edits as we collaborated on this project; Robert Neely, our brilliant editor who can seamlessly pull off miracles; Blake and Pete Berg, who made so much of the content come to life through the layout and cover design; Brandon Schaeffer, Dave Rhodes and Helen Cockram for their various and wonderfully helpful contributions. And to the rest of the 3DM team who made this project possible.

TABLE OF CONTENTS

This is a pivotal moment for the Western Church. Every denomination is in major decline; churches close their doors each week; and, despite all our talk about missional living, many churches flounder and don't know what to do next.

Insert into the midst the church planting discussion. Many believe that the simple solution to this problem is to plant more churches. So we cast the vision, pick the city, recruit the team, raise the money, clarify our branding, and off we go.

Now, several years into the church-planting trend, multitudes of leaders are realizing that the problem is not solved. Creating movements of the gospel is not as simple as good theology, contextualized preaching, or welcoming small groups. Many who launched with burning zeal are now feeling cause fatigue as they struggle to bring the vision God has placed in their hearts to life in real settings. Many simply end up importing older, ineffective paradigms or imitating celebrity pastors' success, and this is often the last thing we need.

So what are we to focus on? How do we move forward to see real renewal in the Western Church, and movement beyond that? Is it better preaching? Is it better facilities? Is it better social media? Is it better programs? As supplemental as these things may be, they all fall short.

I believe that the key for the future of the Western Church is simple, but both profound and hard. The key is a powerful return to Jesus' heart for making disciples, and multiplying them into missional leaders.

Think about how Jesus did his ministry. He preached God's word to the multitudes, but was not seduced by the size and success of the crowds. He demonstrated the power of the Spirit through a miraculous ministry, yet he didn't leverage it for his popularity. He moved on when he could have stayed and built momentum, and he continually prioritized his time, resources, teaching, and attention to a small group of leaders to whom he would one day hand the keys of the kingdom. Jesus said in John 17 that the work Jesus came to do was to raise up his disciples, and his commands to make disciples is the heart of his mission.

But HOW do we make disciples? Even if we agree with the centrality of raising up disciples, how do we form them? What do they need to know, be, and do to continue the kind of ministry Jesus had in mind? And to go a step further, how do we multiply these disciples into leaders who can disciple and unleash other disciples in their spheres of influence?

Enter Mike Breen. Mike is not just a theorist on multiplying missional leaders; he is a proven leader in the field. Mike has written a book that details the proven principles and keys to turn programmatic church on its head and see the heart of God released, as his sons and daughters are equipped and empowered to steward the kingdom of God on earth.

This book is filled with practical, insightful, and theologically sound strategies that will challenge, equip, and empower you to see a movement of missional leaders released in your context.

I believe we all crave to be a part of a movement of the gospel that is bigger than any one personality, church, or theology, that advances Jesus' fame and cause in our world. This book will add great fuel to that cause.

Jon Tyson. Pastor
Trinity Grace Church New York

A BRIEF NOTE
∽ ABOUT THIS BOOK ∾
BEFORE READING:

While this is a stand-alone book, it falls within a content trajectory the 3DM Content Team and I are crafting for the teams of people that engage in our two-year Learning Community process. So this particular book serves, in some ways, as Part 2 after our starting-point book called *Building a Discipling Culture*.

The books follow the trajectory of the Learning Community, each building on the content established in the previous books. They progress in this order:

- Building a Discipling Culture

- Multiplying Missional Leaders

- Launching Missional Communities

- Leading a Missional Movement

Because of this, there are two things we'd like to point out.

First, there will be portions of this book that are a little "dense" and might feel like drinking from a fire hydrant. The reason for this is that we have written and designed this book to be something that you can return to time and time again. It's meant to be more like a handbook and reference tool.

Secondly, you may encounter what appears to be "insider's language" that I use in this book from time to time, especially as it references back to points made in the first book. However, I believe we've made a concerted effort to explain these points so it can be read as a stand-alone book. But to further aid this process, here are a few terms we'll be using throughout the book to establish some shared foundations.

Missional Leader

Someone who *mobilizes* God's people to join his redemptive work in the world

Huddle

A discipleship vehicle for *leaders* that provides support, challenge, training, and accountability and is led by a discipling leader

Missional Frontier

Places or networks of people where there is little Gospel presence and an opportunity for a much fuller in-breaking of the Kingdom of God

Missional Community

A group of 20-50 people forming an extended family on mission together

Character

Being like Jesus (the interior world of a person)

Competency

Doing the things Jesus could do (the external world of a person)

Disciple

A person who learns to **be** like Jesus and learns to **do** what Jesus could do. Therefore, a disciple is someone whose life and ministry reflect the life and ministry of Jesus. Dallas Willard puts it this way: *Discipleship is the process of becoming who Jesus would be if he were you.*

UP/IN/OUT

As we see in the Gospels, Jesus had three great loves and thus three distinct dimensions to his life:

- UP: Deep and connected relationship to his Father and attentiveness to the leading of the Holy Spirit

- IN: Constant investment in the relationships with those around him (disciples)

- OUT: Entering into the brokenness of the world, looking for a response individually (people coming into a relationship with Jesus and his Father) and systemically (systems of injustice being transformed)

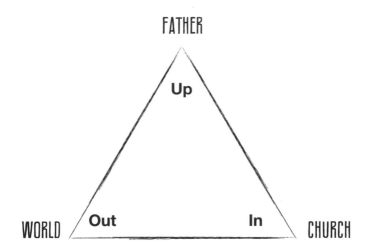

This three-dimensional pattern for living a balanced life is evident throughout Scripture and needs to be expressed individually and in community life.

INTRODUCTION
A TALE OF TWO CITIES

I remember, as a young man, coming out of college. I had done my training in churches as an associate, and it came time for my first call as a senior pastor. As Sally and I were thinking it through, we got the invitation to go to some of the best churches around. But we sensed the Lord say, "Go to the poor. Live in the inner city."

It was an enormous wrestling match for us. And finally, as always seems to happen, the Lord won out. We went to what was, at the time, one of the poorest communities in all of Britain, a place in London called Brixton Hill. The church there was tiny and just trying to survive, and we were the new leadership.

We did everything we could to prepare for the post-apocalyptic minefield that was inner-city London at the time. We brought missionaries and young people with us. We raised as much money from people who had it as we could. But while we arrived with a team ready to get after it, our illusions of ministry were quickly shattered.

Our first instinct was to immediately retreat across the drawbridge. We were facing things like watching our next-door neighbor having his car petrol bombed. (If you don't know what that is, it's a Molotov cocktail that makes it look like the car has had its own personal Hiroshima). Why did this happen? Because our neighbor hadn't paid a debt. Believe it or not, walking around the neighborhood and seeing flaming cars wasn't an unusual experience for us.

We didn't even know how to respond to this kind of environment.

The Lord spoke to us and said, "Look, I want you to be compassionate, but I want you to be strategic. I want you to find out and understand where the people are." So with the few people we had, we started knocking on doors and asking questions. Instead of deciding what it was that our church and our team should do "to them," we decided to ask our neighbors what they'd like us to do "for them."

As we got strategic, we asked people two questions. First, we asked what the worst thing about living in this community was. Second, we asked people if they had to pick one thing for us to do, what it would be. As you can imagine, we got all sorts of responses to the second question: Children's programs. Something for teenagers. Racial harmony. Better transportation. Opening local shops. The list went on and on. There was no real agreement on that one.

But in that first question something surprising rose to the surface. About 97 percent of the people said the same thing about what they liked least about the community.

Litter.

Litter.

Let's put this in context.

This place had the highest infant mortality rate in all of Europe. People were beaten senseless on the streets and left in their blood daily. Robbery and rape and brutality were everywhere. Petrol bombs. Illiteracy. Unbelievably high unemployment.

Litter on the streets? Seriously?

But there it was. Litter on the streets.

After poring over 600 surveys, we came back and just looked at each other. The overwhelming desire from the community was for someone, anyone, to do something about litter on the streets. We prayed about it and thought about it and felt that the Lord seemed to be saying something about Brixton Hill.

Let me try to capture the message we heard: This community was what is known as "sinkhole" housing. It was almost all government-subsidized housing — the projects. The only way to get out was to buy your way out (no one had any money) or trade your way out by going to other public housing that was nicer (and no one was going to swap). As a result, the people there felt like they were in the bottom of the trash can and they were never going to get out.

The people of Brixton Hill felt like the dirty gum stuck to the shoe of the world, like the scum of the earth. Their surroundings told them every day that this is what they were, because there was trash absolutely everywhere.

Maybe that's why they told us they wanted us to do something about litter on the streets.

A community down the street had started doing these things called Marches for Jesus, and so in imitation and innovation of this idea, all 40 of us in the church started doing a Praise and Litter March. After church on Sunday, we ate our packed lunch and got a ghetto blaster. Remember those? It was a stereo that was basically the size of a Buick. It had a tape recorder with giant speakers. We strapped it to a baby stroller that my kids had recently vacated and decorated it with balloons.

BALLOONS. I have no idea what that was about.

Our march was led by our balloon-festooned ghetto blaster on a stroller, playing a recording of me on my 12-string guitar and my buddy playing an upright piano, moving down the street. And it was absolutely awful. *Terrible.* As we pushed all of this down the street, everyone looked at me to lead the singing. After all, it was a Praise and Litter March.

Now in England, if you're having a march, you have to have a policeman there. So the bobby (as we call policemen in England) was walking alongside of us, watching me and expecting me to really go after it. I was singing, but it was barely audible. You could barely hear it.

Eventually, we started to get more into it. We started to break out the garbage bags and buckets and bins to collect the trash as we walked down the street singing.

Eventually, the curtains in the nearby homes started twitching.

We could see the curtains start to open as people looked to see what in the world was going on. Then people started to come to the doors. Finally, a man with a Cockney accent looked at me and said, "Oy, Vicar! Vicar! Whatchya doin'?"

(Everyone in Brixton Hill talked like the gecko in the Geico advertisements.)

I went up to him and said, "We're clearing up the litter."

"NO!" (Again, said in that one-of-a-kind hackneyed accent.)

"Yeah," I responded.

"NO!"

"Yeah."

"NO!"

"Well, you know how we took that survey?"

"Yeah."

"You know how we wrote down everyone's reply?"

"Yeah."

"Well we figured out that everyone thought the litter was the big problem. So we decided to clean it up."

"NO!" Then this man called up to his wife: "Hey darlin', come on down here. The Vicar has a rubber glove on!"

Now his wife came down the steps. "Ahhh, Vicar, what are you doing?"

"We're cleaning up the litter."

"NO!"

"Well, you know the survey we took?"

"Yeah."

"Remember how you said you didn't like the litter?"

"Yeah."

"Well, we thought we'd clean it up."

"NO!"

She said, "Wait there, Vicar. We'll put the kettle on and have a cup of tea." So she went inside and called her neighbor, and we had tea. Then, more people came out of more houses, and we had more tea, plus orange juice and cookies for the kids. It was like wartime England in World War II. Some of them started picking up litter, and the march just carried on down the street.

We did this regularly, and it made a massive difference. They knew that we couldn't clean it all up. It was impossible. But we did something. And funnily enough, the local government felt convicted by it and started to send people in regularly to help clean up.

One day, I was out there clearing some glass near one of the kids' playgrounds, and a guy walked over to me and said, "Alright Vicar, I've got it. I've worked it out now."

"What's that?" I asked.

"I've worked it out. You're very clever, you are, aren't you?"

"What do you mean?"

"It's one of them parabolas."

"A what?"

"A parabola. You know, one of those stories that Jesus tells – a parabola."

"Oh. OK. Well, what do you think I'm trying to say?"

"You're doing something to show us what God wants to do in our lives. You're saying that God wants to clean up our hearts."

I was surprised. "Oh . . . ummm . . . yeah!"

"How do I do that, Vicar?"

And it was easy. I just led him to Christ right there.

Our church kept doing things like this: Listening to the people in the community. Finding ways to connect the Gospel of Jesus to their everyday lives. And I kid you not, revival happened right there in one of the poorest places in all of Europe. We led scores of people to Jesus. The quality of life increased. We were seeing things happen that you only read about in Acts 2. I had never seen anything like it. The Kingdom of God was colliding into earth. The future was coming into the present.

But today, if you go to Brixton Hill, there's very little evidence we were ever there.

Why is that the case? That's where the second city comes in.

Fast-forward about 10 years.

After a few years in Arkansas, Sally and I took a position as the senior leaders at a vibrant church called St. Thomas in northern England. It was in a place called Sheffield where about 2 percent of people went to church. Sheffield was a hard place to live, because it was a dried-up steel town where unemployment was astronomically high. Sheffield is a lot like Pittsburgh in both look and feel.

In my time in Brixton, I had almost accidentally stumbled into some principles and practices that came into full fruition in Sheffield. (No one can get credit for this but the Lord.) Pretty soon into my time there, we started experimenting with a missional vehicle that has become known as *Missional Communities*. These were groups of people, about the size of an extended family (20-

50 people), who were bound together in community by their mission and were incarnating the Gospel of Jesus in every crack and crevice of society, becoming a scattered and gathered church. These groups were laity-led, and the leaders decided what their vision was and how the Lord was asking them to be the church to the places he was sending them.

Over time, it all started to pop. Hundreds and hundreds of people were coming to faith. The number of Missional Communities doubled. Then they doubled again. Then they doubled again. A few years after starting this, much to all of our surprise, we had become one of the largest churches in England.
But then something familiar happened again. I felt the Lord asking Sally and I to leave St. Thomas and move to the United States where the next season of our life would unfold before us.

You can see the symmetry, can't you? Revival happened again, and again I was led to leave. The last time I left, slowly, over time, the imprint of the Kingdom disappeared from that little community in London. It was almost as if we had never been there. But the Lord was asking us to leave, and so we did.

But with Sheffield and St. Thomas, it was different.

Seven years after we left St. Thomas, the church has more than doubled in size and is now one of the largest churches in all of Europe. Thousands have come to Christ through Missional Communities, and a missional movement has spread throughout the European continent from this slightly inconsequential city in the north of England. The quality of life in the city has gone up. The city council, which has always been hostile to Christians and which has done everything it could to make life miserable for believers, started giving out grants to the Missional Communities working with teenagers. Why? After studying these communities, the council found that they were pretty much the only things in the city that were able to positively deal with the crime, poverty, and apathy found among most of the teenagers in the city.

All of this was being done by lay leaders who weren't getting paid. They were just missional leaders doing the work of Jesus in the city they'd been called to.

I've thought about the tale of these two cities a lot. What is the difference between Brixton Hill and Sheffield? Both experienced massive outpourings of the Spirit. Both saw something happen like we see in the book of Acts. I left both churches in the hands of very capable leaders.

After thinking and thinking about it, I have only been able to come up with one real difference between Brixton Hill and Sheffield. I can only see one reason that revival was snuffed out in one place while it continued in another. In Sheffield, I learned how to multiply missional leaders who could lead the people of God. It didn't matter whether I (or Paul Maconochie and Mick Woodhead, the remarkable men who followed me) were there or not. The people of the church understood who they were called to be and whom they were sent to. The everyday, ordinary people of God were leading the church.

In Brixton Hill, I was a missionary who rallied the church around my missionary impulse. But it never became theirs. So when I left, they stopped rallying. In Sheffield, I continued to be a missionary, but I learned how to transfer that missional DNA to a small group of people, who then did the same for others, who then did the same for others. A missional revolution began that has now spanned six continents.

I am absolutely convinced this story is not meant to be the exception but the rule. This is supposed to be the story of the Church. This is meant to be your story — a story of shaping and multiplying missional leaders who can lead the people of God to their destiny.

That's what we will seek to do in this book. You will find practical tools that will help you identify, recruit, and develop missional leaders who can then multiply themselves. So join us on the journey from Brixton Hill to Sheffield and beyond — the journey of multiplying missional leaders.

1

THE PLUG-AND-PLAY
➷ PROBLEM ➶

Imagine that it's a Tuesday morning, and that the staff of your church has gathered for its weekly staff meeting. Staff members discuss the weekend service and whether it delivered the message and experience they hoped it would. They discuss the attendance numbers; small group numbers and effectiveness; budget, buildings, and cash flow. You know, the normal staff-meeting routine.

Then, there's a soft but decisive knock on the door. Someone says, "Come in!"

Into the room, dressed in normal clothes, step Peter, Paul, James, Priscilla, Timothy, and Lydia. (Obviously, we're in a hypothetical situation here.) They introduce themselves and say that the Lord sent them to your church to serve in any way they can. They ask, "What can we do? We don't want to be on the stage or anything. You're doing the preaching/teaching thing really well. But we'll do anything else you need. Just tell us what you'd like."

A stunned silence comes over the staff — after all, this is a strange situation. But soon enough, the staff members snap out of it.

"Uhh, well, OK. Well, how many of you are there? Six? Well, let's see. Could three of you be small group leaders? We're looking to start some new small groups, and clearly you'd be great at that. Peter, James, Paul, could you do that?

"Hmmm . . . you know, we lost the person who heads up our First Impressions team a month ago, and it has been a bit lackluster. It has lost the punch it used to have. You know it's important that people have a strong impression of our church within the first 15 seconds when they come to the service. Priscilla, do you mind heading that up?

"Timothy, we could sure use another usher, you look like you could handle that. Lastly, Lydia, I hear you play a mean bass and can sing too. We're down a bass player and would love to have you in the band. Maybe you can even fill in and lead worship from time to time. Are you up for that?"

This is called plug-and-play. This is about having various positions we need filled in the machine of our churches and plugging people into those roles. Now don't get me wrong: there are always going to be logistical needs when the scattered church gathers. That's reality, and we need to attend to that and do it well.

But does anyone really think this is where a church should be using Peter, James, Paul, Priscilla, Timothy, and Lydia? Would this be the most effective use of their time and energy given the skill sets they have? Of course not.

There's a leadership myth out there that systems and structures create leaders in and of themselves. But this hypothetical example shows us how systems can fall short.

Maybe we can think about it this way: If your church were suddenly given 250 missional leaders, would you have any idea what to do with them? Or would you just plug-and-play them in what you are currently doing?

If we are honest, we'd probably admit that most of us wouldn't have a clue what to do with missional leaders. Chances are they'd actually intimidate us because we wouldn't know what to do with them.

I think this reveals a deeper truth. Our lack of experience with missional leaders shows that, like me when I was in Brixton, most of us have no idea how to shape and multiply missional leaders. We like the idea of it, but our not knowing what to do with them shows that we've had next to no exposure to them. That says something about us.

We read about Peter, Paul, and the others in the New Testament who were starting and leading missional churches and movements, but somehow we haven't come to grips with the fact that this is what we're supposed to be doing too! The types of leaders we read about in Acts are the types of leaders we are supposed to be shaping and releasing. But somewhere along the way, we settled for a different normal.

What if creating and multiplying these kinds of missional leaders was normal for your church?

THE PLAYGROUND

As I've thought about it, it's as though we as churches have taken the leaders of our church and put them in a playground that is just 10 feet long and 10 feet wide and enclosed by a tall fence.

We put these leaders on the playground and tell them to play. That may sound good, but there are a lot of them in one place, and it's pretty crowded. Because the space is so small, there is only room for a swing set, a short slide, and a little merry-go-round. People take turns playing, but they spend most of their time waiting around, wondering when it's going to be their turn. The fence of the playground is so high that you can't see over it. As a result, the leaders don't even know that this playground is situated right in the middle of Walt Disney World. There are a lot of rides and a lot of fun to be had just on the other side of the fence… *and they don't even know it*.

However, I have a sneaking suspicion that if we took the fence down to let the leaders see what *could be*, almost all of them would stay in that small playground. Why? They know that playground. It's what they've always known. They like the swing set, the slide, and the merry-go-round. Space Mountain? The Tower of Terror? The Teacups? They've got no idea what to do with those. Walt Disney World is way too foreign and looks more than a little scary compared to the playground they have always known. So chances are, even if you took the fence down, they'd never leave the playground. And that's the leaders!

This leads to another painful reality.

I would argue that our churches don't have *missional leaders*, but I'd take it a step further. I also think that most of our churches have next to no *leaders*.

Sure, we have leadership development programs. We have dinners, classes, meetings, and maybe even some training. But leadership means that we've been given a vision from the Lord for ourselves and given the power and the authority to execute this vision. This isn't what is happening in our churches.

That's because in most churches, we don't have *leaders*; we have *managers*. We have people who are executing and managing the vision of the few (or the one), not people who are implementing the visions the Lord has given them. Usually we have one genius with a thousand helpers. And to plug-and-play those helpers, we have manager development programs.

Let's be quite clear. In the Western church, there are very few leaders in churches, but there are lots of managers. *What we desperately need are more leaders whose lives and ministries look like the life and ministry of Jesus.*

Bill Hybels was right that the local church, as the body of Jesus, is the hope of the world, but that's not true about the churches we usually see around us, which tend to mimic corporate business models.

If you run your church like a business, efficiency replaces effectiveness. Many churches are organizationally efficient, but we aren't affecting the lives of people the way in which Jesus imagined or hoped for.

We've created a corporate America-like church, and it's because we buy into a false dichotomy between a *leadership culture* that produces leaders and a *discipleship culture* that produces disciples. Here's what I mean: In American businesses, the goal is *moving people* from A to B, but has nothing to do with *making people*. We have one guy with the vision and a culture of volunteerism to help that one guy get his vision accomplished. He's the genius with a thousand helpers. So while churches may claim to have leadership development programs, what they really have are volunteer pipelines. People go from being spectators to volunteers to managers as they get more involved, but they never become missional leaders.

You see, I am absolutely convinced that 100 years from now, many books will be written on the phenomenon that is the late 20th Century/early 21st Century American church. And I am fairly certain that it will be with a large degree of amazement and laughter that people, in reading about it, will say to each other: "You must be joking! Seriously? People actually thought it was a good idea to structure the church as if it were a *business*? Honestly?"

And so, in this so-called leadership culture, we run the campus, but we don't expand the Kingdom. We're keeping the machine of the church running (which, much to some people's chagrin, really is needed if it can be done in a lightweight and low maintenance kind of way), but we're not making Kingdom impact beyond our extraordinarily well-run playground.

This isn't to say that there is a "right" kind of church, or that I'm trying to pigeonhole churches into certain boxes. It's to say that when we look at scripture, it seems that the characteristics expressed in that *Movemental Quadrant* of Strong Discipleship and Strong Leadership are what we see in the healthy, vibrant churches in the Bible. **It isn't that churches finding themselves in the Corporate or Organic Quadrants are "bad;" it's simply I think they could be more effective with more elements of the other in which they are lacking.**

My guess is that most of us find ourselves in the top left quadrant that depicts the corporate expression of church. We have churches that are great at moving people to do things, but are pretty poor at making disciples. Instead, they create a culture of volunteerism that is implemented and run by managers of the leader. This produces very little change inside or outside of the four walls of the church. We protect what we have and don't generally expand the Kingdom.

On the other side, we have organic churches that are great at making disciples, but not terribly effective at mobilizing these people into God's mission in the world. It's just a bunch of individuals running around on their own. (Again, I'm over-generalizing to get the point across.) Perhaps they try to step into mission, but without a clear vision of how they will do that together as a family. When things get difficult, they falter and buy into the false belief that they can be disciples without being missionaries.

What we need is a way of making and moving people so that, as we make disciples, we release them into their destiny of pushing into new Kingdom-frontier. This is what movements do, and we're after a movement of the Kingdom of God, aren't we? *This is why we so desperately need missional leaders — people who can lead us outside the safe confines of the church building and into the world that Jesus so loved so that his Kingdom may expand.*

We need to take down the fence and give people permission to lead. This means that we have to help them hear from the Lord, shape them to be missional leaders like we see in scripture, and release them with the authority and power to do the things the Lord is asking them to do. This is what multiplying missional leaders is all about.

So let's begin to dig into two key questions:
1) How do we create, shape, train, and multiply missional leaders?
2) How do we release these leaders intentionally and purposefully, under a broad vision, so that God's Kingdom advances as a missional movement begins?

Plug-and-play just won't work for missional leaders. They understand their primary role as outside the confines of the church building. They need a big backyard. They need a space to go and grow.

2

✧ THE MISSIONAL LEADER ✧

As we begin to get off the playground, we need to take a moment to lay out the terrain of mission, missional leadership, and discipleship.

Here's what we need to understand right from the beginning: Missional leadership is not simply discipling individual people, but is leading larger groups that disciple and train leaders in a cohesive, organized way for God's mission in the world.

Strictly speaking, yes, you are leading anyone you are discipling because leadership is influence. But the way we want to talk about leadership is through the eyes of *missional leadership*, the ability to mobilize the people of God to do his mission in the world *together*.

My experience tells me that while you can try to mobilize a small group of people into mission (say, perhaps, anything less than 12-15 people), this is often ineffective and difficult to sustain. It's usually small enough to care, but not large enough to dare. So I would say, first and foremost, a Missional Leader is someone who can lead and mobilize at least 20-50 people (about the size of an extended family) or more, because I believe that's the minimum number of people needed for healthy, vibrant, sustainable mission. (We have written a whole book on this called *Launching Missional Communities: A Field Guide*.)

Can someone still be a missional leader and lead less than 20? Of course. But for the purposes of this book we are going to focus on those leading, training and mobilizing a minimum of 20-50 people.

So let's be quite clear about what I mean when I say *Missional Leader*: We mean **someone who mobilizes God's people to join his redemptive work in the world**. Furthermore, I would argue that the most effective missional leaders do this by creating a system of relational discipleship through being in an extended family on mission (more on this later in the book).

Often in this book, I will talk about the *missional frontier*. What I mean by that is a place or network of relationships that need a much larger Gospel presence. The missional frontier is where much more of the Kingdom of God is needed, not through cultural manipulation or culture wars, but through a constant and faithful witness to Jesus and his Kingdom.

You can be a disciple without being a missional leader, but you can't be a missional leader without being a radically committed disciple. So a missional leader is first and foremost a follower, because he or she is following Jesus as a disciple, while also submitting their lives to those who hold them accountable, providing support, challenge and encouragement.

To quickly sum up, I believe these are three crucial aspects of Missional Leadership:

1. Leaders are allowed to hear from the Lord themselves about a vision and are given the authority and the power to do something with that vision.

2. They have the grace to lead *at least 20-50* people into mission together.

3. They are radically committed disciples, with both the character and competency of Jesus, so they are actively discipling others.

Biblical leadership is based on discipleship. This means that, while we may have the skills to move some of God's people together in unity through a shared vision, we can never abdicate our responsibility to make disciples of those whom we are mobilizing. Either we must disciple them personally, or we need to help shape a relational system that disciples them.[1]

MISSIONAL LEADER:
Someone who mobilizes God's people to join his redemptive work in the world

MISSIONAL FRONTIER:
A place or network of relationships that need a much larger Gospel presence

....

[1] We have found the 8:6:4 Huddle Structure to be an incredibly helpful system for doing this. For more information on the 8:6:4 Huddle Structure, read Chapter 4 of *Building a Discipling Culture*

So in order to better understand the nature of a missional leader, let's first explore the nature of a disciple, because a missional leader must embody all of these characteristics. While our previous book *Building a Discipling Culture* covered quite a lot of ground on discipleship and making disciples, the following few sections will provide fresh perspective on this topic and how it relates to missional leadership.

I'm doing this because, as I just commented, you can't be a missional leader without being a radically committed follower of Jesus first. So as we begin the journey of multiplying missional leaders, we must spend some time digging into discipleship, as it must and always start here if you are a Christian leader.

MOVING THE GOALPOST

Defining a disciple is fairly easy, in my view. The Greek word *mathetes* is the word that scripture uses for "disciple," and it means *learner*. In other words, disciples are people who LEARN to be like Jesus and learn to do what Jesus could do. One great writer on discipleship, Dallas Willard, put it this way: *Discipleship is the process of becoming who Jesus would be if he were you.*[2] A disciple is someone who, with increased intentionality and passing time, has a life and ministry that looks more and more like the life and ministry of Jesus. Disciples increasingly have Jesus' heart and character and are able to do the types of things we see him doing.

We don't have to look far in the New Testament to see this happening. Just look at the life of the disciples and apostles and the communities they led. Over time, they looked more and more like Jesus.

How did the church go from 120 people in an upper room to more than 50 percent of the Roman Empire in the course of about 250 years?[3] Simple. They had a way of reproducing the life of Jesus in disciples — in real, flesh-and-blood people — who were able to do the things we read about Jesus doing in the Gospels. And these disciples did this on purpose.

Is that still the baseline we see for all Christians, *or have we moved the*

....

[2] Dallas Willard: http://www.dwillard.org/articles/artview.asp?artID=71
[3] Please see Rodney Stark's seminal book *The Rise of Christianity*

goalpost? I have to wonder if we have changed our criteria to match the kind of fruit our communities are producing. If this is the case, then we are fine with Christians who show up to our churches, who are generally nice people, and who do some quiet times, tithe, and volunteer. Maybe they even have a little missional bent to them. These are all good things, but I don't think this is the kind of fruit Jesus was referring to when he talked about fruitfulness in John 15.

Would those kinds of people change the world like the early church did? Probably not.

In truth, I think we are pretty bad at making disciples in the Western church. Why? I look at the life of Jesus, the life of the disciples, the life of the early church, and what they were able to produce with their fruit — and then I look at ours. When we read in scripture about the texture of their lives and ministry, do we think that ours holds up to it? Even if we have a growing church, do the lives of the people we lead look like the lives of people we see in scripture?

That's the goalpost we should be going after.

I've heard Dallas Willard say that every church should be able to answer two questions: First, what is our plan for making disciples? Second, does our plan work? I believe most communities have a plan for discipleship. I'm not convinced many plans are working the way Jesus is hoping they will — and that's why we're in trouble.

The fruit of our lives will reveal the root of our lives. In Brixton Hill, the fruit of my time there was revealed. It was fruit that blossomed for a season, but in the end, it didn't last. It's not just that discipleship wasn't in my DNA or that I didn't know how. It's that it wasn't something I even put as a priority. I was about building the church, not about making disciples. The fruit revealed my root.

If we are aiming to create disciples and we see a sizable gap between the people we see in scripture as the rule and the people around us, we must ask ourselves why this is the case and how we can change that reality.

"I'LL HAVE A CHEESEBURGER WITH NO CHEESE, PLEASE"

Undoubtedly, one of the key components to being a disciple is caring deeply about mission. Disciples see bringing more of the Kingdom through themselves as one of their primary callings on earth.

In Christendom, it seemed that people thought of discipleship as only an "inner" reality that sought the transformation of the individual while leaving mission on the sideline. As we have come to re-embrace the *missio Dei* — the reality that the God of mission sent his Son as the great rescuer and that we are to imitate him — I wonder if some longing for a "missional movement" are far more concerned with being missionaries/reformers than with seeking the transformation and wholeness that Christ is offering them personally. As Skye Jethani said, "Many church leaders unknowingly replace the transcendent vitality of a life with God for the ego satisfaction they derive from a life *for* God."[4]

Look, I'm not criticizing the people who are passionate about mission. I am one of those people. I was one of the people pioneering Missional Communities in the 1980s, and I have been doing it ever since. This is my camp, my tribe, my people. But it has to be said: God did not design us to do Kingdom mission outside of the scope of intentional, biblical discipleship. If we don't see that, we're fooling ourselves.

Mission is under the umbrella of discipleship. It is one of the many things that Jesus taught his disciples to do well so that it became an integrated reality of their every-day lives. But it wasn't done in a vacuum. It didn't happen outside of knowing Jesus and being shaped by that relationship in which a constant refinement of their character happened alongside of their continued skill development (which included mission).

As a disclaimer, I'm talking about discipleship and mission as if they are two separate things right now. They aren't. They are one and the same. However, because so many people have treated them as if they were, I'm using this as a starting point.

The truth about discipleship is that it's never hip and never in style because it's the call to come and die. It is, as Eugene Peterson says, a "long obedience in the same direction."[5] That's just not very attractive for people in a consumer

....

[4] http://www.outofur.com/archives/2011/07/has_mission_bec.html
[5] Taken from Peterson's book of the same name

culture. While the missional conversation is imbued with the energy and vitality that comes with Kingdom work, it seems to be missing some of the hallmark reality that those of us who have lived it over time have come to expect: Mission is messy. It's humbling. There's often no glory in it. It requires you to be in for the long haul. *And it's completely unsustainable without a holistic understanding of discipleship.*

As I asserted earlier (and also explained in the book *Building a Discipling Culture*), we're pretty bad at making disciples. You can see why this is a huge problem when it comes to launching something missional. Think about it this way: **Sending people out to do mission is sending them out to a war zone.** When we don't disciple people the way Jesus and the New Testament talked about, we are sending them out without armor, weapons, or training. This is mass carnage waiting to happen. How can we be surprised that people burn out, quit and never want to return to the missional life (or the church for that matter)? How can we not expect that people will feel used and abused? And when people see all this happening, is it surprising that when we take down the playground fence, people choose not to leave?

Discipleship is not only the boot camp that trains them for the front lines, but also the hospital where they recuperate when they get wounded and the off-duty time they need to rest.

There's a story from World War I of how the Czar's army sent wave after wave of untrained, practically weaponless soldiers into the thick of the German front. They were slaughtered in droves. Why did the Red Army do this? Because the generals knew that eventually the German soldiers would run out of ammunition, creating an opportunity for the Red Army to send in their best soldiers to finish them off. The first wave of untrained soldiers was the best way of exhausting ammunition and thus leaving the enemy vulnerable.

While this isn't a perfect analogy, I sense this is largely where we are in the "missional" movement right now. We are sending bright-eyed civilians into the battle where the fighting is fiercest without the equipping they need not just to survive, but to fight well and advance the Kingdom of their Father. What we need are missional leaders who can train, mobilize, and lead the people of God to their destiny.

What concerns me is that we have gone ditch to ditch between discipleship and mission, as if, somehow, these two things could be separated. Let me explain. The reality of living more fully in the Kingdom of God is that we are being put back together through God's grace, conforming more to the image of Jesus, and having his heart and mind. The overflow of all this leads to Kingdom activity and mission (though, admittedly, it isn't this linear). That is why Jesus says, "Apart from me, you can do nothing."[6] **Apart from the active work of Jesus in our life, we cannot produce Kingdom fruit.**

Engaging in Kingdom mission without being equally attentive to our own personal transformation through relationship with the King is like asking for a cheeseburger with no cheese. It stops being the very thing we're asking for!

By the same token, being a "disciple" while not actively engaging in mission as a way of life is asking for a cheeseburger with no burger. Both are necessary. **To be a disciple is to be a missionary, and to be a missionary requires that we be disciples.** We must avoid the ditches on either side and travel down the straight and narrow road on a journey that includes the tension found between the two.

CHARACTER AND COMPETENCY

If we look at things objectively, we often see churches with discipling cultures that focus mainly on the transformation of individual self, and we also see churches with missional cultures that focus on the transformation of the world and of the people around us. We often see tensions between these two camps. Here's why.
One has a clue, but no cause. The other has a cause, but no clue.

High mission/low discipleship church cultures have issues with Biblical literacy, theological reflection, and deficiencies in character and creed that, in the end, sabotage the very mission they're about. Critics are rightly concerned that these kinds of churches are a hair's breath away from heresy, with people largely not experiencing the depth and transformation of heart and mind Jesus invites us into. They have a cause but no clue.

High discipleship/low mission church cultures have strength in the previous

....

[6] John 15:5

issues, but lack the adventurous spirit and heart of compassion and Kingdom compulsion that so stirred the Father into action that he sent his only Son to a world he so loved. Their transformation isn't leading to the place God is taking them. Critics are rightly concerned that these kinds of churches will turn into Christian ghettos, creating people who lob truth bombs over the high, secure walls of their playgrounds, thus creating an "us vs. them" mentality. They have a clue but no cause.

In both cases, something is disastrously off. As humans, we are creatures of overreaction, choosing polarities rather than living in tension. The truth is that a true discipling culture (as Jesus envisioned it) must have both transformation of the individual and mission. It cannot live in either ditch. It's not either/or; it's both/and. We should never choose between depth and breadth; instead, we must embrace the tension of having and shaping both discipleship and mission in our communities and in our leaders.

At the end of the day, we can probably boil being a disciple down to two things: **Character** and **Competency**. We want the character that Jesus has and we want to be able to do the things that Jesus could do (which is competency.) *Discipleship is learning, over the course of our lives, to become people who have both character and competency.*

So think about the average leader in your community.

- **Character:** Are their lives characterized by grace? Peace? Love? Transformation? Patience? Humility? A deep relationship with the Father? A love of the scriptures? Can they submit? Do they see the world through the eyes of the Kingdom and not the prevailing culture? (Obviously there's a lot more to character, but you get the idea.)

- **Competency:** Can they disciple people well who can then disciple others? Can they do mission well and see their everyday lives, not just events, as a mission field? Can they hear the voice of their Father and respond with action imbued with his authority and power? When they pray, do things happen as they did for Jesus? Can they read and teach scripture well? (Again, Jesus was able to do many things; this is but a short summary.)

These are Kingdom questions. And if you think through this filter, you'll see why I make the point that if you make disciples, you will always get the church, but if you're really about building a church, you won't always get disciples. If the people in your community are discipling people who can answer yes to the questions above, you're doing what Jesus asked you to do. You've sought first the Kingdom, and the rest will be added.

I find it helpful to look at character and competency through this matrix.

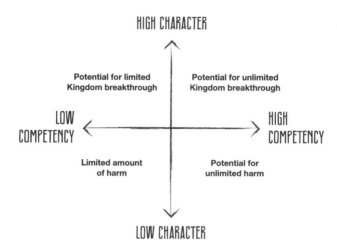

These ideas of character and competency each ask a root question. For character, the question is: *Are you being faithful?* God has asked you to be a certain kind of person and to find your identity in him and not in what you produce or have. He is asking you to do the right thing even when it's hard and to find peace in your relationship with him, both in your present reality and in your future. Are you being faithful to that calling? In the Kingdom of God, success is measured by one thing: Faithfulness through obedience. God controls outcomes; we choose, through his grace, to be obedient.

But we don't just want to be obedient. We also want the Kingdom to win. We want heaven to collide into earth and to see the Kingdom of God more and more present in our current reality. Yes, the battle has ultimately been won, but God is already seeking the restoration of all things and we are part of that. We want that to happen, not for our sake, but for the sake of this broken world and the people we love in it. Because of that, the question we ask in terms of competency is: *Are you seeing fruit?*

If the word disciple means learner, then we can learn to do the things Jesus could do. Through the Holy Spirit, the longer we do them and practice, the better we get at them. That means we see more fruit as we are more in tune with our Father and the practices he gave us through Jesus.

Someone who starts playing golf starts off with a pretty awful swing. With enough practice and enough time (faithfulness), the swing gets better and more consistent, and someone *learns* to play golf well. The same is true of competency within the Kingdom. We don't start off good at very much, but over time, with practice, and as we listen to the Father, we start to get better at Kingdom things.

Are you being faithful?

Are you seeing fruit?

It's here that we often see more ditch-to-ditch thinking. In reaction to many current streams of evangelicalism that largely revolve around attendance, many people have jettisoned asking the question about fruit. They rightly are concerned with being faithful and being obedient, but they seem largely at peace with very little Kingdom breakthrough in their community. Somehow they've equated faithfulness with little fruit.

I am at peace with having no fruit and being faithful and leaving outcomes to the Lord, but make no mistake: *I want fruit, and fruit that lasts!* I want to see the Kingdom come to earth *today*. So if it's not happening, I'm going to be asking why! "Father, what can I be learning? Where am I not very good at something that you're calling me to get better at? What do you want to teach me?"

You see, we can't get real Kingdom fruit out of our lives without faithfulness. But in being faithful, we should be working for fruit and expecting it. We should be laboring toward that end, humbly learning and seeking to be better at Kingdom things, and allowing the Father to sustain us for that life.

Faithfulness and Fruit.

Character and Competency.

Missional Leaders must live out of these realities. For them, mobilizing God's people into mission outside the walls of the church is one of the competencies or the skill sets they will learn over time, but one that must be matched with the strength of their character.

ICEBERG AHEAD

The way that Jesus described it, there is an inner world and an outer world, and the two are connected. There's the life we are living with Father that no one can really see, and there's the external life that people can see.

Among Jesus' many stories, he uses a parable about the outside of a cup and the inside of a cup to describe this reality.[7] The inside of the cup represents what happens inside of us that no one can see and the connection we have with our Father — character. We've probably all heard the quote, "Character is what you do when no one else is looking."

Now the outside of the cup is what happens outside of us that people can see — competency. Jesus seems to suggest that the only way the external world is of the Kingdom is if what is inside comes from the *overflow* of the internal world, a world that he is shaping in us as we are in relationship with him.

Think of an iceberg. When you see an iceberg, you are only seeing, at most, 13 percent or so of the whole iceberg. The other 87 percent is submerged underwater, completely out of view. But the 87 percent you can't see provides the buoyancy that keeps the 13 percent you can see afloat. **That larger, hidden portion is sustaining and holding up what can be seen.**

Jesus is suggesting that the same is true of us. If we want to be missional leaders and multiply missional leaders who see unbelievable things happen — the kinds of movements we've only heard rumors about in other parts of the world or read about in the book of Acts — we need an inner world to support that external fruit. In fact, our chief concern must be the inner world, living out of a place of sustained connection with the Father. That is why Jesus says apart from a connection with him, we can bear no Kingdom fruit.[8] Or, as Paul says, "Since we live by the Spirit, let us keep in step with the Spirit."[9]

The problem, of course, is that we've flipped this.

We have become addicted to **doing** and pay very little attention to **being**. Are

....

[7] Matthew 23:25-26
[8] John 15
[9] Galatians 5:25

we more concerned about doing work for God than about being with God? Do we even know how to be with God without thinking about what we're going to be doing *for him* next? Is it possible that we are hoping that all we do for him will somehow define us — which makes life really far more about us than it is about him?

If this is our reality, how can we hope to shape and mold missional leaders who will live differently? After all, how can we really take people to places we haven't been ourselves?

Character. Competency.

Being. Doing.

Inner. Outer.

Faithfulness. Fruit.

So this is what we suggest: Before we can shape and multiply missional leaders, we must first be disciples of Jesus. And if we hope to do this, it begins and ends with character.

So how is character shaped in us? And how can we shape it in others? Let's explore these questions in the next chapter.

3

∾ CHARACTER ∾

Let's spend a little time understanding this *character* component of discipleship and missional leadership.

Often, when people think of character, of being and the inner world, they start to think about what it means to "go deep." From time to time, I hear of Christians who move from one church to another — church hopping — because they say they are looking for a church that will really "go deep." These church hoppers might admit that at one point their previous church offered depth, but somewhere along the way, they argue, the church sold out, started watering down the Gospel and scripture in one way or another, and stopped "going deep."

"We just want really meaty teachings," they say.

I think I know what they mean by that, but my question is this: Do they?

Most of us can agree that what we want out of our spiritual journey here on earth is **transformation**. We want to live increasingly more in the Kingdom of God, in which God and his life are more and more available to us and through us, and then for it to become available to the people and world we live in. Really, that's all discipleship is. The process of discipleship teaches how to live in the Kingdom of God right now, right here, today. That's what is offered to us as disciples of Jesus.[10]

---

[10] It's worth noting at this point that some of my thoughts here are the results of various conversations and emails about this topic with Doug Paul and Ben Sternke and so in many ways, this section is a bit more collaborative.

However, I think the impulse to "go deep" that people often believe shows their character is essentially spiritual boredom that comes from a stalled discipleship life. You know the signs. Maybe we've stopped obeying because it got hard. Maybe we never were truly obeying. Maybe God's voice has gone silent and it's so hard to hear him in this season of life. Maybe we never really heard him in the first place. His presence seems far away. (There are other reasons for these things happening as well, of course — the dark night of the soul, for one example.)

When these symptoms arise, I think people essentially misdiagnose the problem and thus prescribe something that ultimately won't help that much: Learning something new about the Bible. What they're really seeking, I believe, is simple, radical discipleship. They want to live a life full of meaning and significance. They want to become leaders in a Kingdom movement. And they're simply not going to get it by hearing the Word only. They have to do it to get it.

As John Wimber put it, *"The meat is on the street."*[11]

So in order to talk about how character is a key part of being and multiplying leaders who grow the kind of movements that are seen on the street, we must redefine what it means to truly go deep: to put the teachings of Jesus into practice. That's where the rubber meets the road, and where many choose not to go any further.

Too often, what people are seeking in their desire to "go deep" is the *hit* they get from hearing something they've never heard before, whether it's a new idea, a new paradigm, or a new angle. We get a tingly sense when that happens. We like the tingles and we want more of them, because the more tingles we get, the more holy we feel, and (we wrongly assume) the more our character is being shaped.

Richard Rohr hits this kind of thinking on the head:

> *We operate with the assumption that giving people new ideas changes people. It doesn't. Believing ideas is, in fact, a way of not having to change*

---

[11] This is a very common John Wimber quote that he repeated in almost every context he led or preached.

in any significant way, especially if you can argue about them. Ideas become defenses.

If you have the right words, you are considered an orthodox and law-abiding Christian. We burned people at the stake for not having the right words, but never to my knowledge for failing to love or forgive, or to care for the poor. Religion has had a love affair with words and correct ideas, whereas Jesus loved people, who are always imperfect.

You do not have to substantially change to think some new ideas. You always have to change to love and forgive ordinary people. We love any religion that asks us to change other people. We avoid any religion that keeps telling us to change.[12]

I'm not saying people who think this way aren't Christians; I'm saying they aren't understanding the portrait of the Christian life into which Jesus is inviting them. And people like this can never be missional leaders.

We have taught people far beyond their obedience levels. They don't need more information. They actually need to do what scripture says to do! Jeff Vanderstelt put it this way:

Often when I speak to leaders and people who wish we did more Bible studies at (our church community), I ask them what was the last book of the Bible they studied. Let's say they've respond with "James."

I then say something like, "That's great! I'm sure you're now caring for widows and orphans, visiting the sick, caring for the poor, etc...!" To which I generally hear, "Well no...not really." Then, I say, "But I thought you studied James?" "Well, yes, but I'm not necessarily doing that."[13]

As my friend Alex Absalom would say, "The problem with Christians isn't that they don't understand what Jesus said. The problem with Christians is that they don't do what Jesus said." And Jesus was all about reproduction. To use his parable, a mature tree will bear (reproduce) fruit.

As Jim Putnam wrote, "I know many Christians who have the ability to be

....

[12] Adapted from How Men Change: A Thin Time (CD, DVD, MP3) by Richard Rohr

[13] http://www.vergenetwork.org/2011/02/08/how-is-a-missional-community-different-from-a-printable/

spiritual parents but don't make it a priority. Though they would like to call themselves mature, I would say that they are not. Why? Because they have not prioritized their lives around the mission of Christ, which is to make disciples."[14]

GOOD BOYS AND GOING DEEP

The rich young ruler had the kind of impulse we've been talking about. He asked Jesus, "What must I do to be saved?"[14] Even though he was a good boy, something compelled him to go further, to "go deep." He figured this Jesus guy seemed to know a lot, so maybe he would know what else a good boy needed to do.

Jesus teased him a little, I think, by telling him to obey the commandments. It's almost as if Jesus was saying, "Didn't that do it for you?" But the rich young ruler still wanted something more. So Jesus said, "Here's what you're lacking, and what you really need: sell everything you have and come follow me."

The answer was being with Jesus. Jesus didn't want the rich young ruler to merely know about God or the Bible or scripture. He invited and challenged him to come and know God and be shaped from that relationship. The rich young ruler was offered the internship opportunity of a lifetime. (By the way, this kind of internship opportunity of a lifetime is also offered to all of us. Discipleship to Jesus is the best opportunity you'll ever get as a human being.)

But instead of accepting it, the rich young ruler went away sad because he wouldn't part with his wealth. He couldn't get over the idea of giving up everything. There was something fundamentally mis-ordered in his life. Tim Keller described this tendency, which we share, by discussing how Idolatry is when we make a good thing a great thing.[15]

The rich young ruler went to Jesus in search of some kind of "deeper" teaching, but Jesus knew what he really was longing for was the freedom and joy of being his disciple. The rich young ruler wanted the hit of a new idea

....

[14] Excerpted from Jim Putnam's book *Real-Life Discipleship: Building Churches that Make Disciples*

[15] The exact quote is "A good thing among many was turned into a supreme thing, so that its demands overrode all competing values. From Tim Keller, *Counterfeit Gods: The Empty Promises of Money, Sex, and Power, and the Only Hope that Matters* (New York, Penguin, 2009) 8.

from scripture. He knew it all, and he wanted something new. But he got a hit of a different kind as Jesus invited him to real depth. Jesus was telling him: *You're not actually getting the point of knowing the law. Here's what you need to do to fix it: It's about being with me!*

The rich young ruler was interested in the right answers, and he was interested in following God and even "going deep." But he wasn't interested in anything that required him to change his interior world, to deal with the stuff rattling around in there.

This is my fundamental issue with the "go deep" kind of people. If I can make mass generalizations for a moment, I see them this way: They want to go into the endless minutiae of scripture, which can be a good thing, but they rarely really want to do anything with it. They think that knowing about something is the same thing as knowing something. The have bought into the lie that *knowing* more scripture changes you.

It doesn't.

Doing what scripture says and responding to God's voice changes you. This isn't to say that knowing scripture isn't important or that knowing creedal statements and doctrine aren't important. But the point is that scripture is incarnated in you. You read the text and the text reads you. The point is that, because Jesus is working it out in you through your relationship with him, you are the flesh-and-blood embodiment of what scripture says.

Ultimately scripture, creedal statements, and doctrines are statements about what we believe reality is — so let's live in reality! This isn't something we can disconnect or disembody from the way we live. **If you're not actively seeking to live in it, you don't really believe it.**

How does this happen? *It requires a fundamental desire to want to change the broken person that I am and let God's Spirit do his work.* It requires someone who says, "I'm not fully living in the reality of God and his Kingdom, and I'm going to orient my life so that I actually do that."

I have not seen that desire in the kinds of people who say they want to "go deep." They're looking for the hit.
We don't need the hit. **We need to be people who want to be with Jesus for**

the sake of being with Jesus. If we don't want that, why in the world are we Christians, much less Christian leaders? We cannot be missional leaders or multiply missional leaders without being with Jesus and being formed by him.

So how will we know if that's happening, if that kind of character is being shaped in us? Well, scripture gives us one slice of this kind of maturity in Galatians 5. We will notice in our lives and in the culture around us that we are creating (because leaders define culture) that there is striking presence of love, joy, peace, patience, kindness, goodness, gentleness, faithfulness, and self-control. Again, the fruit will reveal the root.

But there are powerful forces working against this becoming reality in our life as missional leaders and in the lives of the leaders we are looking to shape. What we must understand is that everything in our culture is stacked against this becoming a reality in our lives.

INTO THE WILDERNESS

Let's look at one of the Gospel accounts of Jesus' temptation in Luke 4:

> ¹Jesus, full of the Holy Spirit, left the Jordan and was led by the Spirit into the wilderness, ²where for forty days he was tempted by the devil. He ate nothing during those days, and at the end of them he was hungry.
>
> ³The devil said to him, "If you are the Son of God, tell this stone to become bread."
>
> ⁴Jesus answered, "It is written: 'Man shall not live on bread alone.'"
>
> ⁵The devil led him up to a high place and showed him in an instant all the kingdoms of the world. 6And he said to him, "I will give you all their authority and splendor; it has been given to me, and I can give it to anyone I want to. 7If you worship me, it will all be yours."
>
> ⁸Jesus answered, "It is written: 'Worship the Lord your God and serve him only.'"
>
> ⁹The devil led him to Jerusalem and had him stand on the highest point of the temple. "If you are the Son of God," he said, "throw yourself down from here. ¹⁰For it is written: 'He will command his angels concerning you

to guard you carefully; ¹¹they will lift you up in their hands, so that you will not strike your foot against a stone.'"

¹²Jesus answered, "It is said: 'Do not put the Lord your God to the test.'"

¹³When the devil had finished all this tempting, he left him until an opportune time.

Jesus had been commissioned by the Father and filled by the Spirit, and in that anointing he was led away from the Jordan and into Judean desert. It's not that far — nowadays, you can drive that distance in about 30 minutes.

Where Jesus was — most likely in the desert found between Jericho and Jerusalem — there's an aqueduct that took water right from Herod's palace in Jericho into Jerusalem. Clearly Jesus was going to need water if he was going to be in the desert for 40 days without food, so people generally assume this is where he was located for these temptations.

While Jesus was in the desert, the Devil attacked him in the area that was going to be most essential if he were going to stop him in his work: his identity. The Devil knows how to deal with human beings. He has been dealing with them for a long time. So he knew that the place that he had to shake Jesus was in the area of his identity. So the very first place that he started, and the place that we see repeated three times, is with a jab at identity: "*If* you are the Son of God..."

We need to look at the issue of identity, because it is the main battlefield when it comes to character. It is where the Devil attacked Jesus and where he attacks us, and, if not addressed, can sideswipe a missional leader.

So let's look at where the enemy attacked Jesus: Appetite. Approval. Ambition. (I know they all start with the same letter. Why wouldn't they? Alliteration is God's gift to us!) Let's see what these things say about us.

Appetite

When the Devil came to tempt Jesus, the first thing he said was, "If you're the Son of God, turn these stones into bread." He was going after the appetite issue. The enemy attacked Jesus in the area of appetite because our appetites give us a sense of who we are by the definition of need. So *needs* are a component of how we understand who we are.

There are fundamental appetites — appetites for food, sex, shelter, sustenance, nurture, and more. These are fundamental aspects that are trigger mechanisms within the human heart, and they are actually all good things.

By fasting alone in the wilderness, Jesus was addressing one of his appetites — the appetite for food. By saying *no* to one of his appetites, Jesus was dealing with what is necessary to being able to say no to all of them.

A really holy man who leads the Nigerian revival, Enoch Adeboye, said to me one time, long ago, "You know, the church really needs to learn how to fast in Britain. Really, they need to fast so they can say no to certain things and be able to fast so they can remove within themselves the resistance they have for other things through the power of God."

I asked him to explain this further.

He said, "Appetites are like children. If you don't say no to any of them, you'll find yourself overrun. If you learn to say no to one of them, they all hear that, see that, and know that the Spirit working in you is creating the capacity to say *no* to all of them. And actually, by saying no to one of them, you empower yourself to say no to all of them."

If there is an appetite in your life that is not controlled, very often the way to deal with it is through indirect effort. Spiritual giants throughout the ages attest to this. Spirituality is usually through indirect effort. Dallas Willard puts it this way: *"Say no to the things that you can so you can learn to say no to the things that you can't."*[16]

Indirect effort is fundamental to athletic training these days. Swimmers spend far more time in the gym than they ever have before, training muscles that don't appear to have a lot to do with what's necessary for swimming. But that's what prepares them for success.

It's indirect effort.

....

[16] Quoted from the 2010 Ecclesia National Gathering. For more, please see Willard's *The Spirit of the Disciplines*

A lot of times over the years, I've spoken with young guys who have dealt with struggles of pornography, which at this point has reached such levels of infiltration that it's an epidemic. I mean it's *everywhere*. It's almost impossible not to struggle with it. How do you deal with it? It's an appetite. Your body and all of your wiring tell you that you need this. So you have to be able to say no to that need.

But if you simply try saying no to that need directly, it doesn't quite work. It seems to have a certain power over us. So you learn to empower your capacity to say no by dealing with another appetite that is more easily targeted, such as food, through fasting.

For some, food is the appetite you can't say no to. So you need to say no the TV or the iPod in the car. It can be whatever it is for you. Find the place where you can deal with the issue of saying no. Appetite is going to be an area where our enemy tries to undermine our identity because he knows it is such a fundamental need.

If you're going to be shaping missional leaders, you need to know this. With the small number that you are discipling and investing your life into, what are the appetites that control them like little children? How will you help them? How will you hold them accountable?

Approval

Our enemy will also go after our sense of approval. Rather than finding peace in being sons and daughters of the King, people adopted into a family with a loving Father, we find ourselves needing the approval from people around us, desperately hoping they will affirm our value. Maybe we're hoping they like us or that they see us as successful.

Many of us have hung our coat of identity on receiving the approval of others instead of on the love of our Father, who tells us before we ever do anything for him, "I love you. I'm proud of you. I believe in you. I always have and always will."

Look at it this way: Almost everyone I know wrestles with how to best challenge those they lead to live into their Kingdom responsibility. The way you begin to deal with the issue of giving or receiving challenge is by functioning with authority in speaking into another person's life. But if you think you are functioning with authority in another person's life just because you think you have position over them, you're going to come unglued. The authority we have comes from knowing that God already loves us and our identity is set, not because we've been given a title to wield as an instrument of power.

Again, think about being a missional leader. Do you see how the inner world and the outer world are connected here? If your authority to speak confidently comes from the Spirit working inside you as a child of God, knowing that he loves and approves of you, you have authority you can stand on. But if your identity is coming from a position you think you have and your own insight or wisdom, you will get into trouble when leading others.

Most of us are so afraid of what people in the church will think about us when we challenge them to live according to their true identity that we never step into what God is asking us to do. If you wrestle with this issue of challenge or holding people accountable, if you find it difficult to call people to the responsibility and character of the Kingdom and to assume their rightful place by representing the King well, it's because you haven't settled your identity with God. It's an identity thing. Either you believe that you're a child of God and are therefore authorized to represent him in the place he's called you, or you don't.

Now a statement like that (which is obviously challenging in and of itself) will force you back and make you think. The point is that it's supposed to make you think. Where you are seeking approval will absolutely go to the heart of our identity.

Ambition

The Devil tested Jesus in terms of ambition by saying, "Throw yourself off the highest point of the Temple and see if God's angels will catch you."

Recently, I was able to spend time with some dear friends in the Holy Land, and we got to visit a lot of the sites associated with the life of Jesus. In one spot, we looked up at the Western wall. At the very top, the wall extended probably 60 feet beyond where the trumpeter would come out at various times during the festivals. It was the highest point of Temple Mount.

From the top, that was a *long way*. If you jumped off of that and then floated to the ground where the throng of people mingled in the outdoor market, it really would be a sensational start to your ministry! If you started your ministry by leaping off there, and then saying, "Tada!" you'd almost certainly get a book deal and a few Christian conference circuit appearances off of that one.

That's basically what the Devil offered Jesus here. It's like the Devil was saying: "Surely you're ambitious to get this thing going. You've got a job to do. So get on with it!" He was offering a shortcut, not through obedience but through sensationalism. In other words, Jesus was being asked to sacrifice his character for the sake of making a big splash with lots of followers from the very beginning. He was being tempted to start his ministry off with a bang.

Let's look at ambition when it comes to missional leadership. Why do you do the things that you do? Are you doing them out of obedience? Out of faithfulness? Out of love for Jesus? Or does it have to do with your own ambition and your hopes to be defined as a success (whatever you think success means)?

TEMPTATION AND AMERICAN CULTURE

My observation is that these three areas — appetite, approval, and ambition — are temptations to which the Devil always returns, whether in an individual's life, the life of a local church, or even the life of a culture. Clearly the scriptures tell us that our enemy is active and trying to infiltrate every place where his enemy is operating. So he looks to undermine cultures through the subtle insinuation of warped versions of appetite, approval, and ambition.
When I consider this and look at culture missiologically (as an anthropologist), I start to see some patterns emerge – particularly as I look at the United States. So let's think about this. How has the enemy worked where we are and led Americans to put a positive spin on the temptations of appetite, authority, and ambition?

Let's look at these three things in American culture positively first.

In America, you've heard that people should be free to live their life and grow their life in a way that God had designed them to do. Free from the constraints of a feudal system. You should be allowed to fulfill your ambitions that God has put in your heart: life, liberty, and the pursuit of happiness.

How does this show itself in America's history? It means the freedom of the individual. Now in a political sense, it means you are absolutely committed to one person with one vote: Democracy. That's the foundation. But it's so much more than that. You are free to do whatever you are capable of doing. The reason you really believe this is because you've seen the dark image of the mirror you're looking into that is Britain. And you've said, "Look, if that's the alternative, we don't want it."

In looking at England, you see yourself, but it's the image of yourself that is reversed as you are looking into a mirror because this country was founded, in many ways, as a reaction to life in England.

In the UK, there is a mentality of scarcity. Not a lot of land. Not a lot of resources. The expectation that you will always just eke by. In the United States, there's an abundance mentality.

My son and daughter have just built a house in Pawleys Island, South Carolina, where we live. Do you know how rare it is to build a house in England? Here, everyone has the freedom to save money, find their own builder, buy some land, lay the foundation, and build a house. That really is a rarity in England.
In the early years of America, the abundance was so extraordinary that it caused the early settlers to be overwhelmed with giddiness. Just think about this: You're a pioneer coming to a new world and you've finally thrown off the chains of the feudal system in Europe and made it to North America. The village you came from comes to you and says, "We are going to die in the mud here, but we've saved all of our money, and we're going to send you as our representative to the new world."

You carry this money to the freight ship, buy your ticket in steerage, and live below deck. You're sick the whole way. You land in this new territory and someone says to you, "You can do whatever you want."

"What do you mean?"

"I mean you can do whatever you want."

"What will I eat?"

They take you on a boat in a river on the eastern seaboard (and there are scores of accounts of this happening in the early history of America). As you're rowing, you notice that it looks as if the water is boiling because there are so many fish teeming in the water. You lower your coat into the water, pull it up, and there's enough fish to feed you and your family for the week.

"Who do I pay for this?" you might ask. "What are the taxes?"

"You just eat it. Don't worry about taxes," they say.

You walk into the forests and there are so many deer and other animals that you could almost throw a rock and kill something for dinner (well, maybe not exactly). But it had to be absolutely overwhelming. Out on the prairies, you see herds of beasts unlike anything you've seen before that. When they are moving, they take days to pass you and your family by. Days.
It's almost too much.

And there is this thing about Manifest Destiny in the middle of the 19th century when they are literally asking, "Could this be the Kingdom of God?" Whole religions coming out of the United States are premised on it.

That's why abundance is riven into the life of the average American. We see the all-you-eat buffet for $9.99 and think, "Yep. This is good. Life is good."

Life. Is. Good.

In Europe they look at something like that and go, "Ugh." They think it's disgusting. I promise you, they really do! "Why would you want to eat that much?" they ask.

If you look at the early literature of America, such as in Virginia, they would describe the pursuit of happiness as the ability to own land. You go and you stake your claim. It's amazing how many people in the United States want to be entrepreneurs. Even if they can't be. Even if they aren't good at it!

Look at the abundance before you. It's your unalienable right as an individual, as a child of God, to stake your claim and have a go at whatever you decide to put your mind to. That's just how Americans think.

Life :: Abundance.

Liberty :: Individual.

Pursuit of Happiness :: Stake your claim.

In America, the *individual* has authority. It is an issue of freedom. Writers such as John Locke, David Hume, and Adam Smith were some of the thinkers who most influenced the intellectual worldview of the founders. This worldview, which made its way into the culture of the United States, is all about the individual. It says, "You are not under the dominion of anybody except God. You're an individual made by him, equal to everybody else, and you are free to seek a good life." That's the strap line of America. Approval plays out with the individual. This is why freedom and democracy are so important. It is about the empowerment of the individual.

INDIVIDUAL / APPROVAL

For appetite, as we've already seen, the underlying expectation of American culture is *abundance*. The Indians used to watch with fascinated wonder as the Europeans came in and systematically killed everything as they hunted. It was as if they were saying, "Wow, we're not allowed to hunt at home because everything belongs to the king. He's the only one allowed to hunt. In this new world, we are the only ones with guns! So let's all have guns, and we'll all be able to hunt. Let's go kill something!"

You can completely understand it. They had never been allowed to hunt before. They had never owned anything. They had always been massively taxed. Now here was a spread of abundance unlike anything they'd ever seen.

But of course it starts to skew a little. The settlers killed everything, creating heaps and heaps of dead things with all this unprocessed protein. One example is all of the herds of North American bison. No one ate all of the meat. Most of it just rotted in the field after all the bison had been shot. That animal could keep a family alive for half a year, and literally *millions* of them were killed and went to waste.

This shows us how abundance played out in America's early days. So we can picture how abundance became deeply engrained in the American psyche. It's simply part of our culture.

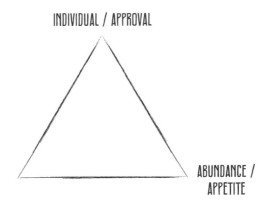

In terms of ambition, in America people got to *stake their claim*. The great reality of America is that there was enough land for everybody. So it's with breathless wonder that you read reports of September 13, 1893, at noon in the Cherokee Outlook in what is now the Oklahoma panhandle. About 100,000 people came for what would be the last land run. Many of them *walked there* from the East Coast. Can you imagine that? They all turned up in time for the race. There were 142 acres for each claim, for a total of 40,000 claims (a total of 6.2 million acres were available for the taking). So there were going to be a lot of disappointed people. Now you understand the story behind the cannons firing as everyone rushed into the distance. Staking your claim is what it was all about.

If you work hard enough, you can achieve whatever you want. That message isn't just for daytime television. Everybody says that.
What has the enemy done in these areas? Let me break down what I see.

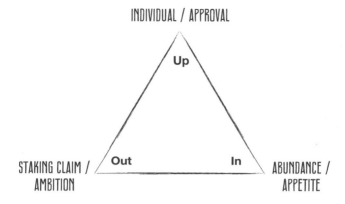

INDIVIDUAL / APPROVAL

Up

STAKING CLAIM /
AMBITION

Out

In

ABUNDANCE /
APPETITE

- The emphasis on the individual has been twisted into the celebrity culture, which is basically the idolization of the individual.
- The assumption of abundance has led to consumerism and the development of the consumer society.
- Staking your claim has become competitiveness.

So America is tempted by the affirmation of celebrity, the appetite of consumerism, and the ambition of competitiveness. In a moment, we'll discuss the dangers of these things.

But first, we must admit something to ourselves: These temptations show up in the exact same way in the American church culture. And it is this culture that is shaping the character of current and future missional leaders. If we don't have the character of Jesus, we can't have the competencies of Jesus. It's just not possible. If we aren't faithful, we can't produce the kind of fruit Jesus is looking for. It's *all* about character. This is simply how clever our enemy is.

TEMPTATION AND THE AMERICAN CHURCH

Forget everyone else for a moment. What has the enemy done to the American church? How has the church become ingrained with the celebrity, consumerism, and competitiveness that are results of the enemy's involvement in our culture?

Let's start with *celebrity*. It doesn't matter if you're at a mega-church or a church of 100. The pastor is a celebrity. Mega-churches just have more famous celebrities.

And honestly, here's what we must see: The American church thinks this is OK.

Recently I was at a conference with 14,000 leaders in one room. The guy on the platform said this: "Three years ago, I sat up in the cheap seats at this conference, sitting up there in the upper decks, and I prayed that God would put me on the main stage. And here I am. I am proof that God makes dreams come true."

There was a pause, and then everyone started to write down what he'd said as if there was absolutely nothing wrong with it.

Really?

Literally 14,000 people just took it in, wrote it down, and prayed that one day they would be on the main stage.

I was sitting there thinking, "Ummm, are we OK with what he just said?"

This statement sounded normal to all the Americans in the room, but as an outsider who grew up in another country, I'm thinking, "I don't know about you, but I'm thinking the emperor is showing all of his private bits right now!" He was embracing the idol of celebrity and everyone accepted it as OK and perfectly normal.

On to *consumerism*. Think about it this way: It wasn't very long ago that everyone accepted the fact that you build a church by providing people whatever it is that they want. That assumption went completely unchallenged. In most churches, it is still completely unchallenged. How do you build a great church? According to this theory, start with a fantastic, cool-looking, skinny-jean wearing worship leader, add in great teaching, and create an amazing children's program. That'll get people to turn up. If you build it, they will come.

No one batted an eyelid at this assumption. Instead, the church played into it with conferences and books. It was entertainment evangelism. Finally, a very large, well-known church made a very public examination of this principle in their church and realized it just might all be a farce. Up to that point, most everyone accepted that not only was this how you build a church but how you make disciples. You just get people to show up.

Do you see what I mean? These are ways in which the enemy has insinuated himself into our culture *and has gotten us to think that it's OK*. That's how cunning he is.

It carries over in terms of *competition* as well. I've seen many Christian organizations promote the idea that competition between church leaders is good because it helps the church to grow. Seriously.

Say that out loud for a second and think about what it is suggesting. When these organizations get churches together, they calibrate events so that everyone feels competitive with one another and therefore achieve more. I promise you, it is true. I've sat in the boardrooms with them.

Celebrity. Consumerism. Competitiveness. The church is falling victim to these temptations. So let's break down these ideas in more depth to consider what the church needs to do and what you will need to do if you're going to become a missional leader.

As we've said, the idea of *celebrity* is deeply woven into American culture and values. All you have to do is look at the ridiculous nature of reality TV, and you see how Americans are constantly craving celebrity — either being one or finding one whom you can follow and watch and even stalk. (Hello Twitter, we're looking at you.) Now, there is nothing dark or sinister about celebrity in and of itself. You can't make the argument that says Jesus wasn't a huge celebrity in his day.

However, the problem with celebrity comes when we ignore the difference between being *famous* and being *significant*. If Jesus was famous, it's because he was doing something significant. The problem in the church is that many pastors make decisions, develop personas, and define success from the lens of what will make them a famous celebrity. (Often they don't even realize they are doing this.)

In American church culture, it's pretty easy to become a celebrity. You just have to grow a huge church. Now all in all, it's not terribly difficult to grow to be a giant church if you have the right tools at your disposal. *But that doesn't mean the ends justify the means of getting there.* Although Jesus was a celebrity in his day, he was willing to say things that ran people off in droves. In fact, the gospel of Mark (from the middle to the end of the book) chronicles the way that people kept leaving Jesus to the point where, by the end, virtually no one was left. No one wanted to be associated with him for fear of the consequences.

Being willing to say things that run people off is not something we see too often in American churches in our day. I suspect that's because deeply imbedded in the American psyche is the desire to be a celebrity. American pastors are very susceptible to this.

Many subtle things happen with people who desire this kind of celebrity status. They can disengage community and isolate themselves, setting themselves up for moral failure. They can make decisions that are numbers driven and not always Kingdom driven. They can skew to a shallow understanding of the Gospel as opposed to a holistic one that leads people to discipleship. They can put the good of their church (their personal Kingdom) over the good of God's Kingdom.

Think about the culture you are shaping as a leader. *In what ways are your decisions influenced by a subtle undercurrent of a hope for celebrity status?*

Now, let's spend some time examining *consumerism*. It is absolutely everywhere in America. We live in a culture that revolves around consuming. Every TV commercial, every store, every credit card company, every bank, every TV show or movie, every piece of clothing, car or product, every website, every restaurant …every *everything* is tailored to fit your desires, needs, or personal preferences.

No wonder we are so easily infuriated when things don't happen exactly as we want them to happen. We exist in a place that implicitly says: "We are here to serve you and meet your every whim and desire. Let us take care of you." What's more, it's never enough. Eventually the house or the car gets older, and we want a new one. The clothes aren't as fashionable, and we want something that's more in style. That restaurant is getting boring, so we must find another. Our favorite TV show is wearing thin, and the search begins for the

THINK ABOUT the culture you are shaping as a leader. *In what ways are your decisions influenced by a subtle undercurrent of a hope for celebrity status?*

next favorite. It goes on and on and on. *This is how we are wired to think in the United States.*

This idea is backed up by this rationale: *You're worth it.* You deserve to have what you want, how you want it, when you want it. For the most part, the church plays this exact same game. We do the best we can to provide as comfortable an experience as humanly possible, using every means at our disposal to attract people in and then keep them in. We tailor what we do around the consumer's wants and desires. That's Marketing 101, right?

The problem is that, at the end of the day, the only thing that Jesus is counting is disciples. That's it. He doesn't seem to care too much about converts, attendance, budgets, or buildings. It's about disciples. And, by nature, disciples are producers, not consumers. Yet most of our churches are built around feeding consumers. I'd argue that 90 percent of the church's time, energy, and resources are linked to feeding consumers.

But there's a huge issue with this: The means you use to attract people to you are usually the means you must use to keep them. In other words, if you use consumerism to attract people to your church, you most likely must continue using it to keep them, or else they will find another church that will meet their needs. That consumer mentality is antithetical to the Gospel and to the call of discipleship.

Think about the culture you are shaping as a leader. *In what ways is your church community using consumerism as the means to draw people to a Gospel that is, in and of itself, anti-consumerism?*

THINK ABOUT
the culture you are shaping as a leader. *In what ways is your church community using consumerism as the means to draw people to a Gospel that is, in and of itself, anti-consumerism?*

Now let's turn to *competition*. You will never find a more hyper-competitive culture than you do in the United States. As a foreigner living in this land, I can attest to that with the utmost respect. Americans love to win, they love the struggle of the journey, and they love holding up the gold medal of victory.

Now don't hear me wrong: there's nothing wrong with being competitive. It's just that competition has become warped and twisted within our culture. And at least in the church, we are competitive about the wrong things.

Much of the American church finds itself competing with the church down the road. "Are we bigger than them? Do we have more influence than them? Do we have the biggest and best youth group in town? Do people like to get married in our church building? Do people like our church better than theirs?"

The fact of the matter is that there is a battle, we have an enemy, and we should be competitive — but against our enemy! We haven't seen how crafty he is. This seems to be the strategy the enemy has chosen for the American church: "I'll let a good chunk of your churches grow... just not at the expense of my territory." What happens as a result? According to one statistic, between 80 to 90 percent of church growth is due to transfer growth instead of churches striking into the heart of our enemy's territory.[17] We consider it a win because we have the new service or program that is growing, but that growth is mainly from people coming from other churches. That's not a win! That's a staggering loss!

Furthermore, many pastors don't think we've won until we've won *and* someone else has lost. Seriously? For sure, we have an enemy and we should be competitive, but we should be competing against our enemy, knowing that the final battle has already been won, instead of competing against our own team members. Our enemy is so gifted and skilled, so conniving, that he has convinced us that beating the people on our own team is victory while he stands back and laughs, rarely having to ever engage in conflict to protect his territory. He is beating us with a sleight of hand that has turned us against ourselves.

Think about the culture you are shaping as a leader. *In what ways are you competing (both in actuality and simply in your mind) against people who are on your own team?*

A SEARCH FOR SOLUTIONS

So let's be clear. I'm not talking about general society. I'm not talking about typical American culture. I'm talking about the American church. My question is this: What are we going to do with these things?

THINK ABOUT **the culture you are shaping as a leader. *In what ways are you competing (both in actuality and simply in your mind) against people who are on your own team?***

---

[17] Statistic from *Stealing Sheep* by William Chadwick

It's going to be really difficult to win against our enemy using methods that are not thoroughly Biblical and oriented toward Jesus. I would say the real issue with the celebrity-centered, consumer-driven, competitive church is that most people never meet Jesus.

That's the real problem.

Who cares if someone looks good on stage? God bless the skinny jeans. Fantastic children's work is great. Killer worship bands are great. Beautifully sculpted teachings are wonderful. I'm pleased for you if your church has these things. But the real issue is whether your church is shaping people who look next to nothing like Jesus or the kind of believers we read about in the Bible. We have to come up with something that deals with the cultural realities that we face or we will find ourselves, yet again, falling into the traps and temptations that Jesus faced at the very beginning.

How can we build something around the freedom of the individual and not lead to celebrity? I suggest that a word like *movement*, where individuals can find their place in a greater body of people but still be free, is a place to start. *Unique, but not independent.* That's because movements are not defined by celebrities. A movement, by its very nature, is a movement of people who are being sent. To coin a phrase, it's about *sentness*.

How can we build something to combat consumerism? I suggest that being a *producer* rather than a *consumer*, that being *fruitful*, is a really important way to understand how to live in an abundant world.

When we say be a producer, what are we really saying? We're saying be a disciple, because Jesus defines a disciple as someone who can produce good fruit. A fruitful person is a disciple, and a disciple is clearly not a consumer.

Lastly, how do we deal with ambition without being hypercompetitive? I suggest that the whole thing about ambition and staking your claim could be dealt with if we took the language of *mission* as our normal, everyday vernacular about our expectation and lifestyle. This is a battle and we are supposed to be trying to win. We are supposed to be ambitious, and we are supposed to be competitive, but honestly, we have a big enough enemy without worrying about any other Christians. Competiveness should drive us to mission, to battling for Kingdom expansion (though not through "cultural Christianity").

So these are some potential solutions:

- The individual should be about movement, not celebrity.
- Abundance should lead to fruitfulness, not consumerism.
- Ambition should play out as mission, not competitiveness.

All of these begin and end with identity, and identity is not something you conjure up within yourself. It is something given to you from an outside entity. We need our identity to come from an unshakeable, unwavering place. We need it to come from our Father who says, "You're my kid. I love you. I believe in you. I am yours and you are mine. Nothing can ever change that."

AMNESIA

The funny thing about identity is that we tend to forget who we are. We find ourselves more and more defined by the things our culture wants to define us by than by the fact that we are the sons and daughters of God. Thankfully, scripture has a keen understanding of our forgetfulness and gives us some strong ways of remembering whose we are and who we are.

The Psalms often speak about the writer getting up early in the morning and seeking after the Lord. The Gospels constantly record Jesus getting up early, before the rising of the sun, and going to quiet and secluded places. The interesting thing about these "secluded" places is that the original Greek word used there is the same word used in Luke 4 to describe the "wilderness" where the Spirit led Jesus before the temptations happened. It's as if scripture is suggesting that *every day* our first battle is to travel back to the wilderness, to the place of wrestling with identity, to relocate who I am and whose I am. Every day we must be reminded, "This is who you are!" Every day we wrestle with identity, and every day there is an open invitation to have our character refined in the wilderness, where there is only our Father to sustain us. The wilderness is where no one else can see us, where our Father reminds us that we are his dearly loved children and that nothing can change that. I don't know about you, but that will change the way I walk through my day.

Another way God helps us remember is through the celebration of the Lord's Supper. In 1 Corinthians 11, Paul says: *For I received from the Lord what I also passed on to you: The Lord Jesus, on the night he was betrayed, took bread, and when he had given thanks, he broke it and said, "This is my body, which is for you; do this in remembrance of me."*

The Greek word for remembrance is the word anamnesis, which is where we get the word *amnesia*. Here, it is trying to say "anti-amnesia." What Paul is literally saying in Greek is this: "When you take the bread and wine and celebrate the Lord's Supper, do this so you don't forget who you are!" We celebrate communion, mass, Eucharist, the table (whatever you call it) because Jesus knows how we operate. He knows we are forgetful. He knows how easily our identity is shaken. He knows that his death and resurrection, which is what we are re-enacting with the Lord's Supper, is what solidifies that covenant identity for all time.

Remember whose you are and who you are.

If you will seek the Lord, if you will make knowing him and being known by him your primary aim, not only will your character be shaped into the likeness of Christ, but you will also be building the foundation for missional leadership, both in your life and in the lives of the people you are shaping.

This foundation of character is what sets the table of competency. To see how, once again we turn to Luke 4.

PHYSICS

At the beginning of Luke 4, we see that, "Jesus, full of the Holy Spirit, left the Jordan and was led by the Spirit into the wilderness, where for forty days he was tempted by the devil."[18] As we have seen, Jesus was tried and tempted, and his character was forged in the battle for his identity.

What happened next? "Jesus returned to Galilee in the power of the Spirit, and news about him spread through the whole countryside."[19]

....

[18] Luke 4:1-2a

I don't know that I can ever make a bigger point on the connection between the interior world and the external world than what we see right here in the life of Jesus. The Spirit led Jesus into the wilderness, where a wrestling match for the identity of Jesus took place. Jesus won the battle; his identity was solidified, and he left *in the power of Spirit*.

Do you see that? Did you catch it? Winning that battle of identity is what gave Jesus the authority and power to go begin his public ministry. His authority came from knowing that the blood of the King flowed through his veins. He knew that royal blood gave him authority and that he had the power that comes with it.

You have the same authority and power. You are a kid of the King, and royal blood flows through your veins. If your identity is found in Christ, then that is where your confidence and authority comes from.

Luke tells us that Jesus had "the Spirit without measure." The issue, of course, is that we don't see that in our lives. That probably means we don't see that in the lives of the people we lead if it's not present in our own lives. So what's going on here?

We'd suggest it's physics: P=V/R

This is a fairly simple physics equation. Power=Voltage/Resistance.

$$P=V/R$$

Voltage is the key. Voltage is about potential. If the Holy Spirit represents *potential*, then we know there is unlimited potential because, as Paul tells us, "the same Spirit that raised Christ from the dead is now living in us."[20] It's the same Spirit! The same Spirit that rested on Jesus coming out of the wilderness, which he had without measure, is within us. So what gives?

Resistance is what gives.

The power that we see in our lives is completely dependent on our resistance

[19] Luke 4:14
[20] Romans 8:11

(or lack thereof) to what God wants to do in us and through us. In other words, the more of "us" there is, the less power there is. If loads of celebrity, consumerism, and competition are rooting around inside of us, that's a *lot* of resistance. The result is next to no power of the Kingdom advancing through us.

If all of that is rattling around inside of us, blocking the Holy Spirit from his work, *this is fundamentally about character*. This is why I've spent so much time on the interior/exterior world, temptations, icebergs, etc., at the beginning a book on multiplying missional leaders. It's all about character. If you don't have the character of Jesus, you simply can't sustain the continued work of his Spirit as a missional leader who multiplies missional leaders. It's just not possible.

Look at it by working out the equation to the other extreme. If we have resistance equaling zero, then we will have the infinite power of God. But that requires no resistance in us. We see this clearly at work in Paul. He constantly talked about emptying himself (less of me, more of Christ), being poured out as a drink offering, and more. He said things like, "His power is made perfect in my weakness."[21] What do we see happen? You know, nothing that crazy. He had a handkerchief. People took it around, and everyone who touched it was healed. That's not really that unusual for someone who had as little resistance as someone like Paul.

In Acts 16, Paul was stuck and frustrated on a mission trip and had no idea where to go. Every time he thought he knew where to go, the Spirit blocked him. His missional plans were foiled. Out of nowhere, he saw someone in Macedonia (which was in Greece) saying, "Please, come help us!" Boom. Off he went to Greece, where there was an open door.

When you have very little resistance and when you are learning Kingdom competency, there tends to be a lot of Kingdom fruit. But it starts with character.

Where is there resistance in your life? What won't you do? What aren't you seeing that is blocking the Spirit from working? Where are you trying to be strong as the Lord needs you to be weak? Where are you getting by on your

....

[21] 2 Corinthians 12:9

own strength as the Lord is asking you to let him do it?

These are questions we must answers as we move from character to competency.

4

~ COMPETENCY ~

In our world, the standard view of leadership suggests we should always play to our strengths. So we specialize in one task or one way of working or one hobby to the exclusion of others. The result is good work in one area but no work in another.

But this is not the way that God wants us to live as missional leaders. Instead, missional leaders must embrace the paradox of the Kingdom. The life of the Kingdom that Jesus lays out and that Paul fleshes out even more suggests that spending time in places of weakness is key to maturity in Christ and to being a missional leader. Playing within your weaknesses produces something good in you while replacing places of darkness and brokenness that can't produce things of the Kingdom.

In my previous book *Building a Discipling Culture,* I discussed Ephesians 4:11-13 in great detail. While I don't want to go too far in depth here based on what we've already written, there is an excerpt we need to wrestle with again.

Each of us has a base ministry that represents one of the fivefold ministries in Ephesians [Apostle, Prophet, Teacher, Evangelist, Pastor]. We believe that God gives each of us this ministry and it is ours for life. Hence, we call this our "base ministry." But there are also particular periods when God leads us to discover and understand the other ministries for a brief time. This is what we call our "phase ministries." We all have our base and at least one phase ministry at any given time. For example, the Lord may call you to teach a class on reading the Bible that you may not necessarily feel most comfortable with. Perhaps your base ministry is a Pastor, but you sense God calling you into a "phase" of being a Teacher. Your base ministry will be the one that refreshes you, the one you are most passionate about. The Lord, however, will mature you by taking you through each of the other ministries in phases. It has been the experience of many that the Lord will make your base ministry more rounded as you experience phases in the other areas.

So one way of understanding Base and Phase is learning that our Base is something that we can't help but do, but God still gives us seasons when we have a Phase of another ministry to learn the basics of it. One of the things that I noticed when I was a young man in my 20s was that I had different seasons of trying new things. I'd have a year or two when I went through a season of immersion into Evangelism, but eventually, the grace ran out and I would just go start something new. Then I'd have a season where I apprenticed myself to someone who was very Prophetic and learned a lot about what it is to act out of that Prophetic ministry, but the grace ran out and I started something new. This happened over and over where God would lead me into a season of learning a different ministry, where I spent a good amount of time in that Phase, but I kept returning to starting new things, which was my Base ministry. I just couldn't help myself. Well, as it turns out, there was a reason for that. I'm an Apostle.

Our general observation is that we enter into Phases for one of two reasons. First, we have a clear sense that God is asking us to learn a ministry we don't yet possess. So while I'm Apostolic in nature, it is crucial that I also know how to be an Evangelist when the situation arises. Being an Apostle isn't an excuse for not fulfilling an important part of the Great Commission. I may not be as good as a natural Evangelist, but I spend time in a Phase so I have at least a foundational level of competence in that ministry. Second, we enter into a new Phase when circumstances arise that immerse us into a Phase ministry we are unfamiliar with, but need to have access to in order to accomplish the work God has called us to. An example of this might be someone with a Pastor Base who has been serving as a Discipleship Pastor at a local church stepping into a Teaching role because the Senior Pastor stepped down. Someone needs to teach, you've been put in the role, and now you have a quick learning curve!

What some people have wrongly assumed is that they should only operate out of a place of absolute strength when it comes to Base ministry. "I'm an Apostle. I'm only going to do things that reflect that ministry." However, Paul clearly does not see it this way. When he says, "and become mature" in Ephesians 4:13, he is referencing the individual arriving at a threshold of maturity, but it is still referencing the various ministries. Maturity, at least as Paul is defining it *in this passage, seems to be an individual having a measure of competency in each ministry, "so that we will no longer be infants."*

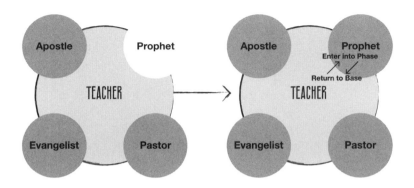

What we end up with is a spiritual formation process that leads us from infancy to maturity, but only when we have spent a Phase within each ministry that is not our Base. Spending time there, in a place that isn't our natural place of strength, gives us access to these Phases at other times when we will need them. What we soon see when we reach maturity is that we are constantly faced with situations where God is asking us to do his work in the world and our Base ministry is insufficient. While we will certainly be far off from the person of Jesus, God is able to use the seasons of life where we have spent extended Phases learning a different ministry to use us in that specific situation.

Now, we all know many church leaders who stubbornly refuse to do anything but the things they are good at. As we see here, this is a recipe for disaster because it leaves us very deficient in our ability, through the Spirit, to do the things Jesus could do. As the section from *Building a Discipling Culture* concludes:

We are not all called to be pastors, but we are all called to care. We are not all called to be teachers, but we are all called to hold out the Truth. We are all responsible for learning how to listen for God's voice, something that comes more naturally for the prophet. We are all called to share the Good News with others, but this takes all those who are not called to be evangelists out of their comfort zones. And we are not all apostles, but must all learn to walk out into what God calls us to do.[22]

....

[22] For more information on the Fivefold Ministries, read Chapter 10 of *Building a Discipling Culture*

We have all met people who only play to their strengths, haven't we? If Paul is right that "his power is made perfect in my weakness," it should come as no great surprise that sometimes the people who only play to their strengths also have some of the greatest character deficiencies. When we operate out of our phase, it puts us in a position of weakness in which only the grace and power of God can work. Allowing God to be strong in our weakness isn't a sign of leadership stupidity but a signpost of Christian maturity! Yes, it's paradoxical, but doesn't Jesus constantly reference paradoxes when describing life in the Kingdom?

UNDERSTANDING FIVEFOLD

When we grow accustomed to operating in places of weakness instead of in self-sufficiency, God is finally able to use us. As a result, the places we are naturally gifted become places where the Spirit can work. To put it another way, there is far less resistance even in our areas of strength.

If these five core competencies are to be the places where much of our character is shaped as we are stretched to places of weakness in our competency, we had better understand them!

First, understand that the Fivefold Ministries are lenses through which we function, with your Base being the one you find most natural to you. What they do is provide a way of seeing and operating in the world and in the Spirit that God can use in many different ways. For instance, more and more missional leaders are using the mid-sized group of missional communities[23] to create extended families on mission together. The way a Prophet would lead a missional community is vastly different than how an Apostle would lead one. There isn't a "right way" to do it because each functions differently and brings a different lens. But they will start the group, grow the group, disciple people, sustain missional activity, and multiply *differently* than the people who lean toward a different fivefold ministry.

If that's the case, it will prove incredibly important to understand how each of these functions.

The following is a unique way of understanding each Base/Phase Ministry

....

[23] See 3DM's book *Launching Missional Communities: A Field Guide* for more on this subject

among the Fivefold. For each, we'll provide a brief overview of the ministry and then explore how the ministry functions through the relationship with God, the relationship with the Body, and the relationship with the world. Notice that the correct progression is always from Father to Body to World. It *always starts with the Father.**

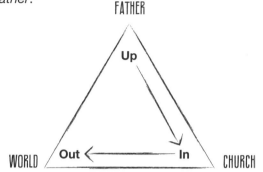

1. Apostle — The Apostle is called to be a **sent one**. Biblical examples are Paul and Peter. In the church, the apostle is looking for what isn't and joining in how God is going to do it. As a result the apostle pursues anything missional instead of the status quo. In the world, the apostle is the entrepreneur, always starting his/her own business.

Core question of the apostle: Are we leading the people of God to their destiny?

 • Correct path: UP to IN to OUT: A fresh vision for new frontier is given and confirmed within the community. New frontier is taken as the whole church works together in unity.

 • UP to IN no OUT: Nothing happens. Lots of new ideas, but very few finished ones.

 • UP to OUT no IN: Vision can change frequently and people stop following because the apostle isn't discerning between a good idea and a God idea.

 • IN to OUT no UP: Good things are happening but with next to no Kingdom breakthrough. Everyone's ideas are being implemented, resulting in a leaderless organization, a lack of a coherent vision, a lack of unity, and a lack of cohesiveness.

....

* You will notice we use the UP/IN/OUT triangle for much of what we discuss and layer into other triangles (as you will see later in the book). The reason for this is we constantly want to be looking at things through the lens with which Jesus understood his life and the world he lived in.

What does it look like to value, create space for, and release these kinds of leaders?

- Create an environment where failure is OK and expected as a byproduct of entrepreneurial efforts.

- Don't just pacify entrepreneurs but welcome and release them.

- Avoid being threatened by new ideas and out-of-the-box thinking.

- Embrace a strong principle of low control with high accountability.

2. Prophet – The Prophet is called to be **forth telling** and **foretelling**. In the church, the prophet is the one most passionate about prayer and worship. In the world, the prophet would operate in the arts as a poet or musician.

Core question of the prophet: Are the people of God hearing his voice and responding appropriately?

- Correct Path: UP to IN to OUT: The prophet receives fresh revelation. This revelation is given to the community to interpret, and the community then produces the proper and appropriate application into action. As a result, hearing from God and responding becomes a communal exercise.

- UP to IN no OUT: This results in *charisma*, as there is lots of spiritual energy but nothing really happens. No one is different as an individual or as a community and there is no transformation to be found.

- UP to OUT no IN: This results in *chaos*. We make the wrong application because we never got the right interpretation. This also creates a proud and arrogant prophet who assumes he/she is always right. This eventually can lead to subversive manipulation.

• IN to OUT no UP: This results in *advice*. There is no real revelation, so the advice is all based on gut instinct.

What does it look like to value, create space for, and release these kinds of leaders?

- Value that God is still speaking.

- Give the prophet the direct invitation they need to feel it's OK to share.

- Create a playful and experimental environment where they are free to "get it wrong."

- Provide appropriate spaces and venues to share corporately.

- Create language for prophets to use to share well so that people can accept or reject. Doing this creates space for an 80/20 response in which you're pretty sure 80 percent of what the prophet says is right, while creating room for the 20 percent possibility that the prophet could be getting it wrong.

3. Evangelist — The evangelist is called to **bring the good news**. In the church, they are all about multiplication. Many evangelists are incredible L1 leaders (beginning leaders) if provided high accountability and given low control. Also, evangelists are often frustrated with the church because they love the world so much and want to see it rescued. In the world, the evangelist is the salesperson who delivers a message about "the best thing ever" that you need.

Core question of the evangelist: Are new people entering into the Kingdom of God?

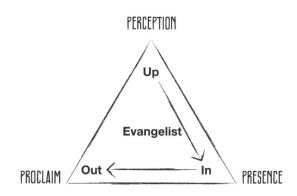

• UP to IN to OUT: You evangelize to people who have been prepared in advance by God (Persons of Peace, as articulated in Luke 9 and 10), and so you see people receive you and become Christians. You also show people you've brought with you what healthy evangelism looks like so they want to do it. This is all done in community, where people see God's Kingdom in a visceral way, so that people are cared for because they are people and not targets.

 • UP to IN no OUT: Nothing happens, except perhaps a social gospel.

 • UP to OUT no IN: Evangelism happens with no incarnation of what the Gospel looks like in a community. People are treated like numbers or notches on the belt. Often evangelists are preaching a gospel of sin management alone.[24]

 • IN to OUT no UP: You end up with lots of angry people who weren't ready for the Gospel and with your people no longer wanting to evangelize. The result is that you're overwhelmed by the tasks of caring and sharing while seeing very little happen. This can manifest in guilt.

What does it look like to value, create space for, and release these kinds of leaders?

- Value the evangelist. If you want to see people come to know Jesus, you have to do this, because evangelists will always want to spend more time with non-Christians than Christians.

- High value on accountability and community for evangelists. You won't see evangelists a lot because they are constantly with people who don't know Jesus yet, so you need to hold them accountable to the life they are living and the way they are leading others. They can also be mavericks and outsiders who spend most of their time outside of the community, so releasing them to be themselves while creating a community they understand is important.

- Find ways to continue to work out the Gospel in a compelling way that evangelists can share.

....

[24] See Chapter 2 of Dallas Willard's brilliant book *The Divine Conspiracy* for more discussion of this idea

4. Teacher — The teacher is called to **hold out the truth**. This is exemplified in Jesus' teaching, because he held out things people had never seen. In the church, the teacher is the mentor and the discipler. In the world, the teacher is the teacher, the trainer, the life coach, and the person who holds out the truth.

Core question of the teacher: Is the Word of God coming alive and being incarnated in the lives of individuals and the community?

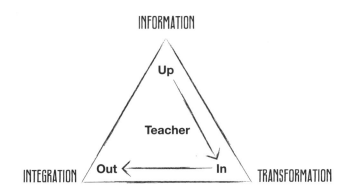

 • UP to IN to OUT: Scripture reveals places for repentance through the individual and the community, and change occurs as we believe and actively step more fully into the Kingdom. It is revelation, knowledge, and wisdom, all together instead of separated.

 • UP to IN no OUT: Everything is theoretical, which leads to hypocrisy. Nothing changes, because you've become the foolish man Jesus talks about in Matthew 7 who hears the word but does nothing about it.

 • UP to OUT no IN: Things are hierarchical, as one person has the insight and everyone else lives it out. Things are about information, not knowledge. As a result there is no sense of calling within community. It is a duty-oriented community, not a loving community, one that lacks the fruit of the Spirit. A high quantity of work is happening, but no spiritual quality of work in the community.

 • IN to OUT no UP: Things are spiritless, which leads to anarchy. Dogma and legalism ensue. Scripture isn't fresh, it is rarely used well or used at all, and God is strangely absent.

What does it look like to value, create space for, and release these kinds of leaders?

- Create a culture of learning where people want to learn as well as do something about it.

- Create more than one platform where teachers can operate.

- Avoid forcing people into the teacher role.

- Acknowledge that a teacher doesn't have to be the teaching pastor. We desire spiritual knowledge and will take it from a variety of places, not just one person. Having a degree of accreditation doesn't make someone the fountain of wisdom.

5. Pastor — The pastor is called to **shepherd** — to lift up the broken, clean them up, and lead them forward. In the church, pastors are not just the pastoral staff but also any who participate in shepherding and caring for others. In the world, the pastor is in the caring professions, such as a counselor, a doctor, or something similar.

Core question of the pastor: Are the people of God showing compassion for the broken and alone?

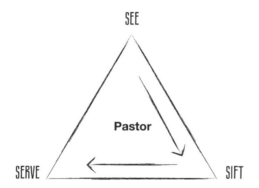

 • UP to IN to OUT: Our hearts break with the Father's. We discern which people God is calling us to serve and then we serve those prepared for us.

 • UP to IN no OUT: Nothing happens, because while there is lots of intention, there is no realization of care.

 • UP to OUT no IN: The pastor constantly serves everyone, and eventually burnout ensues, followed by guilt.

- IN to OUT no UP: This results in the pastor serving from a place of guilt or duty and not from the heart. As a result, service is cold and detached, and it never connects to people's hearts. It feels like doing a job, not a calling, and so the pastor eventually gets angry because serving is usually thankless. Instead, the pastor needs to serve from a place of faithfulness.

What does it look like to value, create space for, and release these kinds of leaders?

- Get out of the mentality that there is one "pastor" who must care/serve everyone. Make room for LOTS of pastors because, from my experience, more than 50 percent of people in churches are pastors.

- Cast vision that the ministry of the church goes beyond the mechanism of the church. Make it clear that service isn't meant to feel like oppression. Call people to serve from freedom, not from a place of guilt or being walked over.[25]

FIVEFOLD AS A LENS

The Fivefold Ministry picture serves as a lens that helps us to understand how people are operating. That's because people from each Base will lead differently based on the lens of ministry they have.

Let's think about this in terms of a few missional vehicles that various churches are using right now:

- Missional Communities
- 24/7 missional prayer rooms
- City serve days
- Classes such as Alpha or Starting Point that help people investigate faith
- Church planting
- Additional worship campus

....

[25] This a key point, because it points to the difference between humility and humiliation. The former is understanding who we are in relation to God and lowering ourselves for others — serving as kids of the King. The latter is another person's vice, because it comes from someone who feels he/she needs to put others down to be exalted. That's slavery, not service.

Someone who leads as an Apostle would start, grow, sustain, and multiply each of these missional vehicles differently than a Pastor would. A Prophet would do it differently than a Teacher. Each of these methods is legitimate, but the differences show how the Base serves as a lens through which each person sees, processes, and understands the world.

So it is key is that we understand that the Body of Christ can only function the way Jesus envisioned it if we have **all five bases** functioning *together*. We cannot focus on one or two to the exclusion of the rest. It's got to be all of them.

To do this, we have to create a culture where we expect diversity of personalities and where we work together even as we see the world differently. In doing this, we as individuals and we as the church of Jesus move toward maturity together.

The lens of Fivefold Ministry is core to the idea of competency, because it helps us begin to recognize how many missional leaders might be among us if we work to develop and multiply them. Even if someone does not have the same Base as we do, he or she can be a missional leader.

As we see people growing in character and competency, how do we recruit them as leaders? How do we develop them? We need to create a pipeline. The next chapter shows us how we can do this.

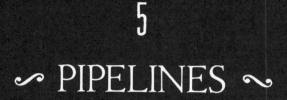

5

✧ PIPELINES ✧

In the previous chapters, we have spent quite a bit of time talking about the quality of a missional leader's life. We've explored the type of character they need to have. We've uncovered barriers they are facing in our culture and in the church. We've highlighted the need for them to have a strong understanding of their Base ministry.

At this point, we now start to turn our focus to the competencies *specific to being a missional leader*.

If you are going to multiply missional leaders who have the character and competency of Jesus, who can lead the people of God into mission, you're going to need a way of doing this that isn't by accident. You're not going to accidentally multiply missional leaders. If you could do it by accident, you'd have lots of them running around in your church, wouldn't you?

As we look at scripture, what we come to see is that both Jesus and Paul had a very systematic way of doing this. We also see that *they didn't do it with very many people*. The pipeline we discuss in this chapter is our way of understanding what Jesus and Paul did to intentionally multiply missional leaders who could then go and do the same thing.

Recruit
Train
Deploy
Review

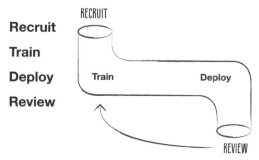

First let's look at the pipeline through the lens of Jesus. (Later, we'll take a very detailed look at Paul, who took these same steps in the book of Acts.)

Recruit: Jesus came out of the wilderness with the power of the Spirit and immediately called 12 disciples to himself to learn to be and to do all of the Kingdom things he could do. He seemed to know whom his Father had already prepared in advance for this task and he called those people to himself.

Train: The disciples got a front-row seat to watch all of the things that Jesus did, and Jesus gave them a running commentary on what was happening as he did it, as well as real-life practice. Their training included trying it with Jesus by their side.

Deploy: Jesus released the disciples to do it themselves. We see this in the famous feeding miracle in Luke 9: "You see a crowd of 20,000 people? Well, feed them!" Also in Luke 10, Jesus sent them without him two-by-two to do all the things they'd seen him do.

Review: After the disciples fed all the crowds, Jesus processed with them. And when the disciples came back from their first mission trip without Jesus, they reported back. In another example, there was a particular evil spirit the disciples couldn't drive out; Jesus gave them feedback.
After they reviewed, the process began again with the same 12 guys: Train; Deploy; Review. He kept sending them out to learn how to be missional leaders: Train; Deploy; Review. **It was the same process for the same 12 guys, over and over again.**

Eventually, though, Jesus sent them out and released them to be leaders in their own right. He ascended into heaven and said, "Guys, I'm never going to leave you. I'll always be with you. But now go and do everything I've shown you and trained you to do. This is the real deal. But don't worry! I'm sending you a helper!"[26]

The point is this: **When left by themselves, they were supposed to do everything that Jesus could do and thus start a missional movement.**

And guess what? They did. And so can you.

....

[26] See Matthew 28:16-20 and Acts 1:1-9

When I left Brixton Hill, I didn't leave a group of missional leaders who knew how to do what I could do as I was leading them. It all deflated when I left because it was based on me and not on a culture of missional discipleship that would far outlast my stay.

Here's the question: *If you left your leaders by themselves, would they know what to do?*

PAUL + THE PIPELINE

One of the remarkable things about Paul is that he had a fairly well articulated leadership pipeline that we can easily follow. It shouldn't be surprising that Paul's version of the pipeline is the same as Jesus'. We begin to see Paul's pipeline starting in Acts 15.

> 15:36Some time later Paul said to Barnabas, "Let us go back and visit the believers in all the towns where we preached the word of the Lord and see how they are doing." 37Barnabas wanted to take John, also called Mark, with them, 38but Paul did not think it wise to take him, because he had deserted them in Pamphylia and had not continued with them in the work. 39They had such a sharp disagreement that they parted company. Barnabas took Mark and sailed for Cyprus, 40but Paul chose Silas and left, commended by the believers to the grace of the Lord. 41He went through Syria and Cilicia, strengthening the churches.

> 16:1Paul came to Derbe and then to Lystra, where a disciple named Timothy lived, whose mother was Jewish and a believer but whose father was a Greek. 2The believers at Lystra and Iconium spoke well of him. 3Paul wanted to take him along on the journey, so he circumcised him because of the Jews who lived in that area, for they all knew that his father was a Greek. 4As they traveled from town to town, they delivered the decisions reached by the apostles and elders in Jerusalem for the people to obey. 5So the churches were strengthened in the faith and grew daily in numbers.

> 6Paul and his companions traveled throughout the region of Phrygia and Galatia, having been kept by the Holy Spirit from preaching the word in the province of Asia. 7When they came to the border of Mysia, they tried to enter Bithynia, but the Spirit of Jesus would not allow them to. 8So they passed by Mysia and went down to Troas. 9During the night Paul had a

vision of a man of Macedonia standing and begging him, "Come over to Macedonia and help us." [10]After Paul had seen the vision, we got ready at once to leave for Macedonia, concluding that God had called us to preach the gospel to them.

This is a fascinating portion of the book of Acts, because we can see the recruiting strategy of Paul and the specific series of filters he used. The passage begins at the onset of Paul's second missionary journey. The first, you will remember, happened when the elders and prophets in Antioch gathered to fast and pray for the Lord's guidance, and the Lord directed them to send Paul and Barnabas out as missionaries. This was the first intentional sending church that we see in the Scriptures, as the leaders of the church in Antioch sent out these missional leaders.

The strategy that Paul and Barnabas adopted is that the leader of the team (Barnabas at the time) went to his home base and begins his evangelistic and missionary work from his home, which was the island of Cyprus. Barnabas' real name was Joseph, but they nicknamed him "The Son of Encouragement" (though I far prefer "Barney"). That's where Barnabas started the work he was called to do.

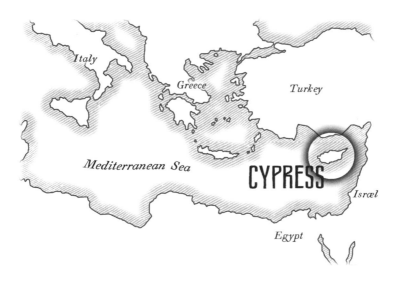

The strategy of Jesus is always the same in terms of our evangelistic and missionary enterprises. You start where you are, and from there you build bridges to the next environment of mission. We see this when Jesus told his disciples to start in Jerusalem, then to go to Judea, then Samaria, and then the ends of the earth.[27] Let's make sure we see how this played out for the disciples.

- If you're a disciple and you go to Jerusalem, you are going to people who are like you and who live in a way you understand.

- If you go to Judea, you go to people who are like you, but they don't live where you live.

- If you go to Samaria, you are going to people who are unlike you, and perhaps even suspicious of you, and who don't live where you live.

If you are going to get to the ends of the earth, you need to learn how to build two kinds of bridges. You build a bridge from the people around you who are like you to people who are like you but not around you. You also build a bridge to people who are not like you, who may be somewhat suspicious of you and who have a very different culture from you. These are usually people who don't live near you.

If you can build these two bridges from the context of your local mission, you can go to the ends of the earth.

So Barnabas followed this simple strategy and went to Cyprus, which we can assume is his Jerusalem or Judea. Then Barnabas and Paul decided to go somewhere quite different. They got in a boat, probably on the northern coast of Cyprus, and sailed north to the coast of Pamphylia. They chose at that point to make a journey into the mountainous region of Galatia.

Pamphylia and Galatia were "interesting" missionary locations —and by interesting I mean as scary as you can imagine. This area, unlike the rest of the Roman Empire, was made up of about *90 percent slaves*. In general, the population of the Roman Empire was about 50/50 between free and enslaved. Remember, the slavery of the New Testament is not the same type that has darkened this continent and besmirched our history. It was much more like

---

[27] Acts 1:8

the indentured servitude of peasants — slaves didn't own anything, didn't have any freedom over their livelihood, and had someone else telling them what to do with every minute of the day.

But this population in Pamphylia and Galatia (originally made up of Celts), which had been a bur in the saddle to the Roman Empire and to previous empires that had dominated this region (such as the Persians and Assyrians), was incredibly fierce. (That's why the Romans gave up, as with the Scots, another Celtic group, and built a wall.) The Romans couldn't negotiate with them, so they decided they were better off subjugating the entire population by taking them into servitude and taking all their freedom away.

So the only way people in Galatia and Pamphylia could be free was by being lawless. That explains why there were so many bandits living in Galatia. According to the accounts of the New Testament era, if you traveled on the roads through Galatia, you would almost certainly be beaten or killed if you did not travel with a large detachment of soldiers or a very large group of travelers. This was a terrifying environment, and to compare cultures today would be similar to traveling the streets of a fundamentalist Islamic nation if you are an American. The locals would attack you, beat you, take everything you have, and strip you, and you'd die of exposure in the mountains.

If you were going to choose your first "Samaria," my advice would be not to choose this one unless the Holy Spirit really told you to! This was a tough mission. Perhaps that's why a young lad named John Mark, a bag carrier for Paul and Barney who was probably no more than 17 years old at the time, decided to go home at this point. (John Mark later wrote a gospel, which probably came from copying down the sermons of Peter.)

Paul and Barnabas continued, even though this was a major loss for their team. (They had just lost 33 percent of their team, leaving them even more exposed and vulnerable as they traveled through this bandit-ridden, mountainous region.) They did their work, planted their churches in Galatia (again, it was obviously far from simple), and returned to Antioch, where a dispute was ongoing. Peter and a number of different leaders from the church at Jerusalem had arrived, and they were now requiring the Gentile believers in Jesus to become Jews by being circumcised and following the Old Testament law.

A dispute ensued between Paul and Peter; we can read about it in the book of Galatians. To settle the dispute, the leaders of the church at Antioch sent Paul and Barnabas down to Jerusalem to get a final word on it from the church leaders there. Meanwhile, the people who had come to disturb the church in Antioch (though not Peter) went north into Galatia and started disrupting the work that Paul and Barnabas had done up in the hill country by telling the Christians there that they had to become Jews as well.

Paul and Barnabas went down to Jerusalem to get the issue settled by Peter and James. In their argument, Paul and Barnabas relied on their testimony of what Jesus had done among them and how the Holy Spirit had led them. They returned to Antioch with a letter to all the churches confirming that they could remain Gentiles.

That moment in the missionary life of the church was one of the most important moments of the early church, second only to Pentecost and the giving of the Holy Spirit. I say that because we probably wouldn't be here now if that hadn't happened. Paul had a huge victory and sent off a letter to the Galatians, one that included some pretty colorful language: "If you're going to get circumcised, why not just go all the way and get castrated?"[28]

THE FIRST FILTER

Having sent that letter, Paul obviously thought he should go and visit the Galatians again, so he suggested this journey to Barnabas. Barnabas wanted to take Mark, but Paul said no chance. We can picture Paul saying, *"There is absolutely no way we can take this kid who ditched us last time when things got hard."*

The dispute probably arose because Mark was sorry. But Paul was not interested. The issue for him was not whether forgiveness was appropriate but whether he could trust Mark. Forgiveness is a gift; trust is earned. No matter what the circumstance in which you find yourself, trust and forgiveness are entirely different realities. Paul simply didn't think Mark was ready for another chance just yet.

From this story, we begin to see Paul's recruiting strategy for missional leaders. We can call this beginning strategy the First Filter. It begins with character and fills out like this:

- **Character:** Does this person have the interior life needed by someone going to the missional frontier, or at least the desire to develop it? Does he or she hear from God and respond in obedience? Does he or she follow through? Does he or she do the right thing when no one is watching?

....

[28] Galatians 5:12

- **Capacity:** Does he or she have the available time in their current season of life to lead something? Is there enough space? Is he or she physically healthy? Emotionally healthy? How does he or she react under stress or when things get hard?

- **Chemistry:** Do you like this person? Do other people like this person? Is this person reasonably good with people? Do you and others enjoy working with him or her? Do you want to go to battle with this person and be down in the trenches with him or her when the pressure is on?

- **Calling:** Is he or she called to this specific work at this specific time?

Now at first glance, this list may not make a lot of sense. Why isn't there any mention of competency? Don't we want them to be good at some things? Shouldn't we take that into consideration? My answer is "yes," but it belongs in the Second Filter of leadership evaluation for recruiting. Again, the issue is that it doesn't matter how much skill, talent, or natural ability you have if you don't have the character to back it up. We are dealing with these first because they are fundamental to how people behave and relate.

Furthermore, I would say that capacity, chemistry, and calling are facets of character, but I have found breaking them up individually makes them easier to understand.

So let's start with calling. Calling is quite difficult to work out, because any person can tell you that they are called to anything. Recently, our 3DM team had to deal with someone who told us they were unequivocally called to work with us. But nobody else sensed that at all, despite that person's certainty. What else can you say? It's a tricky situation. Why are they called? How do they react if you express reservations about their calling? What's their motivation in this calling? These kinds of questions reveal aspects of their character.

Paul also needed someone with the right capacity. He was uncertain about that with Mark, because the only way you ever know about a person's capacity is by finding out when it's empty. You find out the capacity of a person's tank when it's empty, not when it's full. It's about competence based on capacity.

By the way, there's nothing wrong with coming to the end of your capacity. You'll know it. You'll be exhausted, probably teetering on the edge of burnout.

You've reached the end of yourself. What we have to do at that point is to recalibrate our lives along two lines:

1. I need to work within my current capacity

2. I need to ask God to increase my capacity. Capacity can increase, but generally it will never increase until you reach the end of your previous capacity.

So when you're recruiting, spend time with someone assessing his or her capacity. For example, take them on a mission trip or something else unusual to find out what kind of a person he or she is. When you are in a really unusual environment, when you're under threat a bit, you find out realities about character and capacity. Leaders do this not as a Pharisaical judges on someone's character, but simply as a means of trying to assess somebody who will be taking a key role within your Kingdom responsibility. This is a hugely important thing to do. You'll find out key things about character, capacity, and even chemistry in that context. I want to find out through testing a person in the right kind of way whether he or she is someone I want to recruit to be a missional leader on my team.

By the way, this idea of assessment brings up a cultural issue that's worth discussing. One of the problems about Millennials (or Gen Y, the generation right after Gen X) is that people within the generation have, in general, been over-parented. This is a sociological reality that has been studied to death. People born after 1980 have, by and large, grown up in a culture of parenting where parental responsibilities have clutched tightly as a reaction to the absentee parents of the previous generation. The parents we're talking about don't want to force onto their children the wounds that they feel were inflicted by their home life, and so they over-parent their children, to the extent that their children have never been trained to take responsibility.

To back up this broad-brush analysis, simply Google "helicopter parent." You'll find this is a whole new sociological field of research. A helicopter parent is a parent who hovers very close to his or her child all the way into adulthood. Human resource departments are now training their staff to negotiate not only with their employees but also with the parents of their employees. A very common trait in the employment process in the corporate world is that a parent turns up to an interview with his or her child, even though that child is in his or her mid-twenties, to help to negotiate the package for that child. This is so common that HR departments now have to do whole training seminars to deal with this reality.

A person who has been over parented to that extent is, in general, not standing up to the mature adult responsibilities that normally would be associated with the years of development between 20 and 30. As a result, that kind of maturation now doesn't take place until between 30 and 40.

So the development of character and capacity is a huge responsibility. If you are largely working with young adults, know that the vast majority of these adults, even though they may look mature, don't know how to tie their shoelaces. This is such a widespread feature in our society now that it behooves us, whenever we are thinking of bringing someone into leadership, to think through how we can assess that person's character, capacity, the chemistry we might have with them on a team, and through those things, identify and endorse their calling.

If a person is joining a team and does not yet have the necessary character and capacity, I would suggest that your pipeline recognizes that fact and trains people on such issues.

Chemistry is something that is seriously undervalued in recruiting missional leaders. Chemistry doesn't necessarily matter when everything's going well — but you are going to take up arms and charge to the frontier to take on the Kingdom of Darkness! If you can't get along with the person — meaning you can't communicate quickly and take short cuts with this person in the middle of conflict — the whole relationship becomes heavyweight and high-maintenance, which is exactly what you don't want in the middle of a battle.

These things were certainly going through Paul's mind when he was thinking about whether Barnabas was right to bring John Mark along. What he needed was somebody with the right character, and he didn't feel Mark was up to par there.

So the recruiting part of the pipeline needs to be a conscious awareness of the kind of people available in the recruiting pool, and also what we need to take into account in terms of training.

THE JOURNEY CONTINUES

Let's go back to Paul to see how he continued to move down the pipeline. At this point, Paul had left Troas with his team: Silas, a respected prophet from Jerusalem; Timothy, a well-respected disciple from Lystra and Iconium; and Luke, the doctor who apparently was picked up in Troas. (We can surmise this because, from the story of Lydia's conversion on, all of the accounts in the book of Acts are eyewitness accounts by Luke, who wrote the book.)

This was an amazing team to take on the responsibility for mission in Macedonia and Asia. They went through the peninsula of Greece and planted various churches and expressions of God's life in different places. They even left a small church behind in Athens. By the time Paul got to Corinth, his team was scattered throughout the peninsula. They later caught up with him to give him a gift from Philippi so that he could give up the tent-making enterprise he had taken on with Priscilla and Aquila. They were Jews who had been expelled from Rome following an insurrection and who had gone to Corinth, which had become like a refugee camp.

What do you need at a camp for wealthy refugees? People who know how to build tents! Paul was already a member of that guild, and so it was advantageous to his missionary enterprise for him to have that skill-set.

Paul left Priscilla and Aquila in Corinth to do that. He was conscious of the build-up of opposition, but Jesus appeared to him and told him not to be afraid because he had many people in this city.

Keep going.

Paul planted an amazing and significant church in Corinth, and at the end of his time in Corinth he took his Nazarite vow by shaving all the hair off his body, putting it in a bag, and taking it to the altar at Jerusalem as a symbol of himself. As you give up your own self, you ask God for a personal favor. Paul asked God to remove the thorn from his flesh. But the Lord continued to refuse Paul's request because Paul's apostolic calling was much better encased by weakness.

Paul went from Jerusalem back up to Antioch, where he had some R & R, and then he walked through modern-day Turkey. Just imagine! He went through Galatia into Asia, at the center of which was Ephesus, a place he had been trying to reach for a long time.

Paul began his work in Ephesus. Again, he started as a tentmaker, visited the synagogue, and did some teaching. But when the Ephesians became obstinate, he stepped out of the synagogue and revealed his method of training there in Ephesus. We find it in Acts 19.

¹While Apollos was at Corinth, Paul took the road through the interior and arrived at Ephesus. There he found some disciples ²and asked them, "Did you receive the Holy Spirit when you believed?"

They answered, "No, we have not even heard that there is a Holy Spirit."

³So Paul asked, "Then what baptism did you receive?"

"John's baptism," they replied.

⁴Paul said, "John's baptism was a baptism of repentance. He told the people to believe in the one coming after him, that is, in Jesus." ⁵On hearing this, they were baptized in the name of the Lord Jesus. ⁶When Paul placed his hands on them, the Holy Spirit came on them, and they spoke in tongues and prophesied. ⁷There were about twelve men in all.

⁸Paul entered the synagogue and spoke boldly there for three months, arguing persuasively about the kingdom of God. ⁹But some of them became obstinate; they refused to believe and publicly maligned the Way. So Paul left them. He took the disciples with him and had discussions daily in the lecture hall of Tyrannus. ¹⁰This went on for two years, so that all the Jews and Greeks who lived in the province of Asia heard the word of the Lord.

¹¹God did extraordinary miracles through Paul, 12so that even handkerchiefs and aprons that had touched him were taken to the sick, and their illnesses were cured and the evil spirits left them.

We want to dig into this passage in more detail, but first we must acknowledge that this is one of the most amazing missionary stories of history. Remember what was achieved here — in the space of a couple of years, Paul planted a church that became the most important church in the world for the next 400 years. The most important church in the entire Christian world was at Ephesus until Constantine began to drag the church by the gravitational pull of the center of the Roman Empire after the edict of Milan in 313. The Ephesian church didn't lose that status until the Synod of Ephesus in the mid to late fifth century, when there was the big discussion of the position of Mary in the church.

The Ephesian church, planted by Paul, was led by Timothy, and after him, probably by John the Apostle, who was an old man by that point. John came to Ephesus with Mary, an even older woman; she died there, and her grave can be found there to this day. Ephesus was the center of worship for a female deity, Diana. Paul, Timothy, and John all laid an ax to Diana's reputation. External records to the New Testament say that John walked into the Temple of Diana and cursed her idol, and it fell to the ground and smashed into pieces.

This principality, this false god, had been enthroned and worshipped in Ephesus for centuries. It's not surprising the enemy used the church at Ephesus to install a principality back into the church and subvert the singularity of Jesus as the mediator between humans and God.

FROM TEAM TO MOVEMENT

Let's go back to Acts 19 to make sure we see the moment in time when everything changed for Paul.

At this point in his life, Paul was staring mortality square in the face. He had been beaten more times than he could count. He had been stoned. He had been shipwrecked twice! He had almost died of starvation and also of exposure to the elements. His body was probably beyond recognition for everyone who knew him, and he had to be thinking that physically he couldn't withstand much more. He had to be thinking, "If I die, who will continue this? And even if I'm still alive, *isn't there a more effective way, something that's more movemental than one team?*"

This is where the real movement began.

Paul had already planted an amazing church. He had a job as a tentmaker, and in the siesta hours in the middle of the day (probably from 12-4), he rented the Tyrannus Hall, a lecture hall controlled by a man called the Tyrant, who was a fierce professor. At this point, Paul called a team that would evangelize the whole province of Asia. For example, Epaphrus appears to be one of the missionaries who Paul sent out from the Hall of Tyrannus.[29]

We are not sure of all the churches they planted, but we know the whole of eastern Asia came under the sound of the Gospel. We can say with certainty that from Ephesus, a missionary enterprise went out into Asia Minor and

....

[29] Colossians 1:7

that this enterprise planted the seven churches we find listed in Revelation (Smyrna, Laodicea, etc.) along with the churches in Hierapolis and Colosse. All of these churches were planted during that short amount of time. And make no mistake about this: Paul didn't plant these churches — the missional leaders whom he was training, deploying, and reviewing did.

What Paul did, just like Jesus, was deploy people to a specific task. He either wanted someone to represent him (for example, Epaphras and Timothy) or to take care of a specific need in a particular context that required a person who had been well trained (for instance, plant a church).

We find this strategy playing out in Paul's other writings as well. Here are a few examples:

- In 1 Timothy 1:3, we see part of Paul's deployment strategy as he told Timothy to stay in Ephesus. That was a very religious environment, and Timothy needed to take on the task of teaching.

- In 2 Timothy 2:2, we see the strategy for discipleship that Paul wanted Timothy to take on.

- In Titus 1:4-5, Paul demonstrated a very clear deployment strategy. There were things that needed to be done, and so Paul sent Titus — someone he believed would do things exactly the way Paul would, because Titus had learned to imitate Paul's life.

LESSONS OF THE PIPELINE

I suggest that the problem for all of us is that most of our training is not comprehensive enough and that it is way too quick. The culture of the American church has largely borrowed from the corporate world in the way it builds its leadership pipeline. As a result, it's based on this leadership myth: Hire talent and fire people who fail.

That is rubbish, and it's not even close to the New Testament model, which had a pipeline that reflected the way Jesus began the enterprise with his first disciples. The most important part of any missional leader is character, not talent. Second, failure is essential to becoming a missional leader. How else will someone learn? No one was born a great missional leader. You have to learn as you go, which is why the continued review and training is so important.

So how do you create a pipeline that will multiply missional leaders? Here's what you do:

- **RECRUIT** the team with whom you want to start a movement.

- **TRAIN** them on how to pioneer the missional frontier and disciple others to do the same.

- **DEPLOY** your team to cut its teeth in the missional frontier.

- **REVIEW** with them once they've gone out to see what happened and what they learned and to give them practical coaching and spiritual support.

Over and over again, with the same team, train, deploy, review. Train. Deploy. Review.

If you train, deploy, and review long enough with your team, like Paul who went before you, you will be able to release a missional movement of leaders who will do far beyond anything you could ever hope, dream, or imagine on your own. Eventually, you'll be able to release them to become leaders in their own right — leaders who can function in a system of low control and high accountability. Just as Jesus left this world and left his disciples, and felt confident in doing so, so we too can feel confident in sending our leaders out. This is the power of the pipeline.

6

✧ ENGINES + HOUSES ✧

We have seen how the pipeline works, both in the ministry of Jesus and in the missionary journeys of Paul. Now we want to spend a chapter getting into the nuts and bolts of how to use the pipeline. Let's get practical to see how we can shape and release missional leaders who can shape and release missional leaders who then go and do the same.

Remember, the pipeline is:

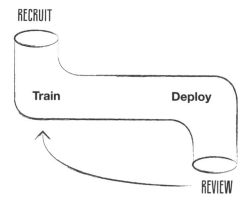

RECRUIT

Train   Deploy

REVIEW

Let's take these pieces of the pipeline one at a time as we get extremely practical.

LESSONS

Who are you recruiting? What exactly are you recruiting them to or for? How do you know which people to choose? How do you know if they are ready?

These questions are probably coming to your mind right now, and that's good, because they are the right questions.

In our previous book *Building a Discipling Culture*, we discussed at length the discipling vehicle called Huddle that we invite current or future missional leaders to be a part of. This is a group of 4-10 people that you are specifically investing in, discipling, and giving your life to. They have access to you in Huddle and outside of the Huddle time together. You will use this exact same vehicle to train your missional leaders, deploy them, and review with them. You don't have to have *another* vehicle (though you can choose to), but you do need to learn to use this one with more skill and expertise as you are training missional leaders.

Remember that having people in a Huddle is not the end game. The end game is missional discipleship, which requires more than the vehicle of Huddle. It also requires access to your life and the life of your family outside of your regularly Huddle time. (Again, you can read much more about this in *Building a Discipling Culture*.)

So how do you know if someone is ready to be trained as a missional leader? First, remember that missional leadership is different than managing an event or program at the church. This isn't management — this is leadership. You are training someone you are discipling as a missional leader to hear the voice of God and to discern where God is sending him or her, and also helping him or her come up with a plan of action to which you will hold him or her accountable. You are sending this missional leader out to the missional frontier, to places where there may not be a Gospel presence, asking him or her to incarnate the Gospel in those places with the teams he or she leads. That is *very different* than how we have seen leaders function in most of our churches, right?

So we need a different process.

First Filter: Character

This process begins, as we saw in the life of Paul, with the first filter. Let's say you have someone in mind that you think has the potential to be a great missional leader. There's something about this person that really connects with the idea of missional leadership in your mind. This is where you start.

We discussed the first filter in detail in the previous chapter. To review, this filter leads you to consider these four things before you think about a person as a potential missional leader any further:

- **Character**
- **Capacity**
- **Chemistry**
- **Calling**

This is the first filter that people need to pass if you are considering inviting them into a discipling relationship with you so that you can train them as missional leaders. My recommendation is that you grade people on each of these four categories from A to F. This is not judging the person or assigning worth; it's evaluating whether they are ready to step into this type of Kingdom leadership. The worst thing that could happen to someone is being recruited and having it turn into an abysmal failure and miserable experience because he or she wasn't quite ready yet. Missional leadership is difficult enough even if you're ready.

So grade a potential missional leader in each of these four categories: character, capacity, chemistry, and calling. **I've found that to pass this first filter, a person needs to score a B or higher in every category.**

Second Filter: Competency

The next filter we are using is about competence. What I've found through the years is that we shouldn't define competency as simply a skill-set someone has or doesn't have. Competency is about skills *and the ability to use those skills at any given time*. For instance, someone may have been a fantastic driver for their whole life, but what if they are drunk? Was the person competent when they drove home drunk? In other words, there are things that can render you incompetent if they are out of control. So with competency, we are assessing readiness (their skill-set) and availability (are they able to use their skills in this season of life?).

If a person sails through the first filter, you'll then want to decide if he or she has the necessary readiness and availability to go to the missional frontier. Let me share a tool that evaluates competency. This is the second filter that I have used for everyone who has ever been on a team with me, for as long as I can remember:

READINESS | NEEDS TO SCORE 80% OR HIGHER

1 = Very Limited 10 = Exceptional	Communicating Content	Leading Communities	Coaching Ability	Connecting Ability	Relationships with Core Team
Demonstratable Skill Level					
Experience in Relation to 3DM					

Overall Readiness	**0%**

AVAILABILITY | NEEDS TO SCORE 80% OR HIGHER

1=Major Hindrance 10 = No Issue!	Location	Family Responsibilities	Financial Commitments	Career Path	Health
Current Realities					
Openness to Change					

Overall Availability	**0%**

This second filter allows you to evaluate where a person already is in his or her development as a leader on several levels. What skills have you already seen in various areas outside of church life? What have you seen in church life? How available is he or she? What is his or her current reality? Is there any give in his or her schedule, location, and family in the near future? This is an incredibly helpful tool in evaluating where people are, and it enables us to accomplish one of our big goals: **Setting people up to succeed as they lead God's people into mission.**

Too often I've seen people who are fantastic leaders and who have all the right skills and training and character to match but are just in a tough season of life. Maybe they've just had a baby. Maybe they are adjusting to married life. Maybe there has been a recent and painful death. Maybe they have a health issue. Maybe they are in a season where there is a project at their job that is taking up unbelievable amounts of energy and time.

It would be a mistake to ask such people to enter into an intentional time of training to release them as missional leaders. This doesn't mean that one day they won't be able to do this, but these are human beings whom God loves, and he is more concerned with them leading from a healthy place than an unhealthy one. God doesn't need us to accomplish his mission; he just prefers to use us. He is ruthlessly committed to us being healthy, and he wants us to make sure we are committed to this too.

This is why we recruit the people who are ready and available.

Third Filter: Be Strategic

I would also encourage you to be strategic in whom you select. Don't hold to this principle with an iron fist, because God can certainly bring other people who you should recruit to your mind. But in general, you should recruit people who are L50 leaders into your Huddle. In other words, recruit people who have the ability to lead groups of at least 50 people. This graphic shows why:

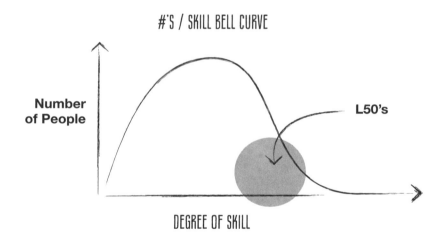

A high percentage of people simply aren't able to lead at least 50 people. So we must be strategic in whom we recruit. Increasingly, as you become a more skilled Missional Leader, you're going to find that your role is to train and equip the leaders of the church to lead God's people into mission. You want to do that with the people who have the ability to do it, because they can make the most of the large amount of time you are investing into them.

Remember, not everyone was part of the 12 with Jesus. Don't think for a second the 72 didn't want to be part of the 12 or that the 120 didn't want to be part of the 72. But Jesus realized a truth that we need to grab onto: We have a limited amount of time and energy, and so we need to spend it as wisely as possible.

How will you know if someone is an L50?

A really interesting story emerged out of the Korean War as the conflict was coming to a close. American generals could never figure out how the Prisoner of War (POW) camps that held American soldiers could only have a few Korean soldiers guarding them when there were hundreds of soldiers inside. How were so few guards able to guard the POWs without having an uprising on their hands?

Finally, one of the Korean soldiers captured by the Americans gave them the insight. When the prisoners were first brought to the camp, an enormous number of Korean guards watched them to ensure there wouldn't be an uprising.

Then, the Koreans sat up in towers overlooking the camp and just watched the prisoners. They ignored age, rank, skill, and physical attributes. They simply looked for those whom people seemed to naturally congregate around. Where were there circles of people centered around one person?

Once the Koreans identified those people, they separated them from the others and put them in solitary confinement. In doing that, they broke the will of the other prisoners. Then the Koreans could drastically reduce the numbers of guards. The L50s (as well as people able to lead more than that) had been removed. Problem solved.

We're not keeping prisoners of war, but this is what we need to look for as well. Become an observer of the people in your community. Ignore all of the things that would keep you from seeing a leader and just observe. Who are people naturally drawn to? Where is there already grace? Where is the Spirit already moving within someone so that people are responding?

Recruit those kinds of people.

TRAIN

In recent years, the question of how to train people has been garnering a lot of attention. I suggest that in order to train the 4-10 people you are raising up to be missional leaders, you will need to know how to do three things:

- Train them the way Jesus and the early church trained
- Multiply yourself into those you are discipling
- Cultivate a culture of learning

If you've read our previous book, *Building a Discipling Culture*, some of these pieces start to come together for you as you're thinking about training missional leaders. But we want to take a moment to break down this process in even more practical detail.

Train them the way Jesus and the early church trained — The Training Triangle

First, we understand training in terms of what Jesus and the early church did. We see this through the lens of Information, Imitation, and Innovation.

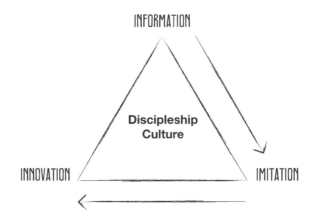

Information we get. We do this well. This is what we grew up on. We give people the information they need to do it. Maybe it's scriptural information. Maybe it's creedal or doctrinal. Maybe it's practical. But we all know that there is information we need to pass on to people because we believe it is essential for learning something.

But then we move to **Imitation**, which is something we aren't as familiar with in the Western church. However, this is something that we often see outside the church. Another word for imitation is *apprenticeship*. Someone knows how to do something that you want to do, and so you apprentice yourself to learn to do what he or she can do. For example, if you want to be a master plumber, you apprentice yourself to a master plumber. If you want to be a surgeon, there is a period of residency where you are apprenticed to a skilled surgeon.

If you want to multiply missional leaders, you will need to apprentice them to do the things you can do. They will start off imitating what you do. You give them important information, and then you show them what that information looks like in the real life by giving them something to copy in your own life.

But it doesn't stop there. It then moves from imitation. For a while someone will imitate and copy what you do, but eventually they come to a base level of competency and can start **Innovation**. They innovate through the lens of their personality. They innovate through the lens of their missional context. They innovate as the Holy Spirit shapes them and leads them. The ultimate point is not that a person looks exactly like you. The point is they start there so they can get to the flexibility of innovation.

So let's think about this practically. Let's say you are training someone specifically to lead a Missional Community, a group of 20-50 people who are a spiritual family on mission together. First, you need to give this person information. What is a Missional Community? What does it look like in scripture? How do they work well? How do you do worship and teach? How do you interact with kids? What about mission? What about pastoral care? These are all very important pieces of information for anyone who is going to be successful at leading a Missional Community, particularly if it's a leader with a 9-5 job that has nothing to do with "church."

But it isn't enough to know the information. You need to see it in flesh and blood. So you take your missional leader and let him or her see how you lead your Missional Community, giving him or her something he or she can imitate. Let's say your Missional Community is incarnating the Gospel in a specific neighborhood that is made up mostly of families with elementary school-aged children. But the missional leader you are training feels called to start a Missional Community that is going to reach out to artists.

This is where innovation comes in. The missional leader you are training will have seen enough broad principles at work in how you led your Missional Community that they can take them, and, even though young families and artists are completely different, be able to innovate what they've learned and seen in their own mission context.[30]

Multiply yourself into those you are discipling — The Leadership Square.

Also, you will need to know how to multiply yourself into the missional leaders in your Huddle. How do they go from knowing virtually nothing about being a missional leader to being able to skillfully navigate the missional frontier and to take new Kingdom ground as the Holy Spirit leads them? How do they go from knowing nothing to missional leadership being completely natural? How do they go from knowing nothing to then shaping and releasing missional leaders themselves in the same way you've done with them?

Well, this is really about understanding how imitation works and how you transfer what you know into someone else's life.

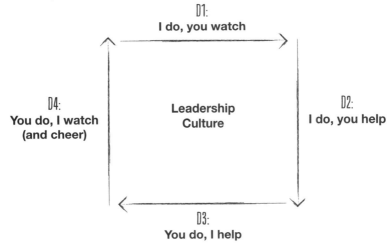

....

[30] For more information on training specific to Missional Communities, please see my book *Launching Missional Communities: A Field Guide*

You want to take a missional leader from a place of unconscious incompetence, where they don't know how to do anything you need them to do, but don't even know they don't know; to a place of unconscious competence, where they can do the things you can do without even thinking about them because they now come naturally.

Simply put, this is how you do it:

- I do. You watch. (unconscious incompetence) — We call this D1.
- I do. You help. (conscious incompetence) — We call this D2.
- You do. I help. (conscious competence) — We call this D3.
- You do. I watch. (And cheer!) (unconscious competence) —We call this D4.

Let's say you're training someone to start, grow, disciple people in, and multiply a Missional Community. This process gives you the lens you need to do this. (Please note how crucial it is for *you* to know how to do this before training others. That's because you will be using your own life as an example when you train them!).

- You launch and start leading the new Missional Community, and the person you're training watches.
- You lead the Missional Community and invite the person to begin helping with various aspects of leading the Missional Community. People see that the person is sharing in the leadership.
- The person begins leading more of the Missional Community than you do, and you help out as needed.
- The person leads the Missional Community entirely, and you only watch and give coaching as needed.

This is what the process of imitation and apprenticeship can look like.[31]

Cultivate a culture of learning — The Learning Circle

The last thing you need for training is to cultivate a culture of learning. As

....

[31] For more information on the Square, read Chapter 9 of *Building a Discipling Culture*

you can see from these last two points, there are endless opportunities to learn new things, make mistakes, experience joy or frustration, mess up, and see massive breakthrough. What we need is a culture where all of these experiences are constantly being processed so that we can learn from them.

You can do this by making the Learning Circle the tool to which you continually return as you are discipling missional leaders and the principle tool you use to review with people.

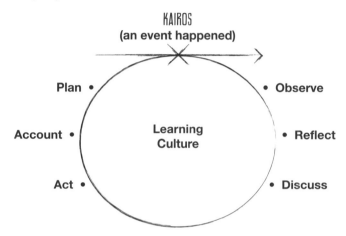

The people you are investing in will fail. They will see triumph. They will see people come to Christ. They will mess up. They will feel overwhelmed. They will feel inadequate. They will see the chains of injustice loosed. They will see things happen that they had only read about in scripture. They will want to quit. They will get tired. They will feel apathetic. They will see all the lights on the dashboard start blinking as they really start to get it.

Each and every one of these experiences is a chance to learn more — more about themselves, more about leading, more about life in the Kingdom of God. When we constantly return to the Learning Circle, no matter our leaders' experience, they will be asking the question, "What is God saying to me, and what am I going to do about it?"[32]

I believe these are three components you must have at work if you're going to train, release, and multiply missional leaders. If we are serious about

....

[32] For more information on the Learning Circle, read Chapter 6 of *Building a Discipling Culture*

training, we have to know how to do it and know if we are doing it well. In my experience, this is how to train missional leaders.

LEADERSHIP ENGINE

I'm a bit of a motor head, and so I have always spent a disproportionate amount of my income and time on cars. I'm always tempted to have nicer cars than I can afford because I love them. I've been messing around with cars all my life, and so when we were writing this book, I looked at the three components we just discussed, and all I could see was a rotary engine. This kind of engine is an internal combustion engine that has only one moving part. It's the most amazing internal combustion engine that has ever been built.

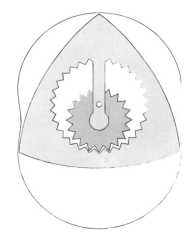

LEADERSHIP ENGINE

The moving part is the crank. The pistons are triangular, and they run around in this square box. Interestingly, the only car that uses a rotary engine today (that I can find, at least) is the Mazda RX7. But, for instance, if you go to the top of almost any oil field, at the top of the machine you will find one of these rotary engines driving the pump. Why? *Because they seemingly last forever.*[33]

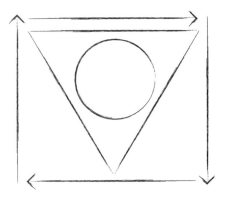

When we combine the three components we just discussed — the learning circle, the training triangle, and the leadership square —we can see that we actually have a rotary engine that runs your leadership pipeline.

....

[33] To see how a rotary engine works, check out this video on YouTube: http://www.youtube.com/watch?v=6BCgl2uumlI

The Learning Circle (which cultivates a discipling culture) holds everything in place, and the Leadership Square doesn't move. Then, the Training Triangle rotates within these two to create the Leadership Culture. Let's think of how this leadership engine works as we try to move a missional leader around the sides of the square from D1 to D4.

D1

When we looked at the Square, we asked ourselves what a disciple in D1 needs to be most successful in this stage. The answer is that we need to lead with information. A D1 disciple needs lots of information on the vision, the plans, and more. A D1 also needs a little bit of imitation so that he or she can tangibly see how this might work out. These are the big things a D1 disciple needs. The last thing a D1 needs to do is innovate because he or she has no idea what he or she is doing at this point. Innovating could be really dangerous.

Picture a person you are developing as a new leader. What does this new leader need the most? He or she needs teaching, training, and input. He or she needs the information and also needs a real-life model of what it is that is being talked about. Information leads, imitation follows.

D2

Let's say our missional leader moves into D2. What does he or she need? What do we lead with, and what comes second? First and foremost, leaders in D2 need a life to imitate, along with still more information. Remember, that D2 is the stage of "I do it, you help," so the leaders need a lot of examples as well as some ongoing instruction as they work to move forward.

We see this in the life of Jesus, when the disciples were down in the dumps and incredibly frustrated. He continued to model things for them, but they still came back around the campfire for Q and A and further instruction. If your leaders are in D2, you will need to give them time, vision, and grace. You're offering them your time, reconnecting them to the original vision, and retelling the information that got them all excited in the first place.

For example, when Jesus called the disciples to become "fishers of men," the disciples really didn't know what they were getting into. They said something like, "Great, we'll become fishers of men!" So off they went with Jesus, and then they basically fell off a cliff, moving from unconscious incompetence to conscious incompetence when they realized that Jesus actually expected them to do all the things he could do!

We can imagine the conversation: "Wait, you mean he was serious? He actually expects us to do all of these things? You must be joking. No way!"

In this "no way" moment, what the disciples needed was a fresh understanding of the vision that had first captured them, time to process, and grace, because there were inevitably going to be lots of questions and doubt. Grace was going to be the means by which they received the fulfillment of that vision. Remember Jesus' words: "Fear not little flock, your father is pleased to give you the Kingdom of Heaven."[34]

After this point, Jesus got away with his disciples, far from the crowds, and spent lots of time with them. This is where the imitation and information took place, all revolving around the discipling culture, spending time with Jesus, using the Learning Circle, and processing what was happening in their lives.

D3

If you're investing in a missional leader in D3, how should you be leading them? What do they need? Imitation is still the primary vehicle you lead with, but the triangle rotates because innovation is now the secondary vehicle. As leaders move into the D3 stage, they are beginning to grow in confidence, competence and a belief they can do the things their leader has been instructing and modeling. They are now starting to ask the question, "How is this going to look in my life?" Innovation starts to happen.

When you have a team that is experiencing imitation and innovation, something starts to happen: They start becoming fast friends! When you have charismatic entrepreneurial leaders coming up with new ideas, new information is easy for them, and they love dreaming up new things. They tend to go immediately to imitation and innovation, expecting their teams to be rapidly innovating all the time. They don't actually spend enough time delivering the new information thoroughly enough (how they got it, where it came from, etc.) to allow all their new leaders to fully engage with them. For you, if your leaders are in this

....

[34] Luke 12:32

stage, the discipline of patiently passing on information must come first.

D4

If you're leading someone who is in D4, how do you need to lead? The leader in the D4 stage leads with innovation, with the second component being information. The reason for this is because now they're doing it and aren't spending quite as much time with you. Sometimes leading in the D4 stage is more about doing intermittent check-ins with information to hear all that's going on.

At this point, your missional leader has been powered through the leadership pipeline by the rotary leadership engine. Now the missional leader is ready to recruit his or her own team and lead the process he or she has just experienced.

DEPLOY + REVIEW

As you can tell from our section on training, deploying and reviewing is a constant reality in the leadership pipeline process. It looks like this:

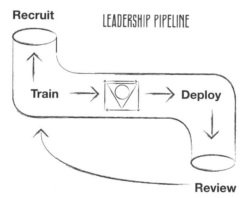

The process is best expressed like this: You recruit your team of current or future missional leaders. You give them some training, as we just described. Then, you deploy them to experience the missional frontier and spend time reviewing.

Then you do it again.

And again.

And then again.

The leadership engine in the training part of the pipeline is so strong that it is able to push people through deploy and review and back into train. These things — train, deploy, review — are going on simultaneously.

Train. Deploy. Review. We see this happening over and over again with Jesus. He trained the disciples. He sent them out on mission trips — sometimes they went with him and helped; sometimes they were deployed in pairs without him. After both of these, they'd come back and review. Jesus gave them more training and then sent them out again. This process repeated over and over. Again, it's just like learning how to do anything, whether it's being a doctor, swinging a golf club, or learning to cook. You practice, practice, practice, and if you practice long enough, with the right training and experiences, you're going to get good!

OIKOS

It's at this point that an interesting thing happens. Up to this point, we've described the three components of the Learning Circle, Leadership Square, and Training Triangle as a leadership engine, which has a certain ring to it, right? But it also has a certain cold, detached feeling. After all, we are working with and shaping real people, and it's hard to talk about a process in mechanical ways when we're talking about people.

I would suggest that something else slowly starts to happen here. You have a group of 4-10 people, and you are all hitting the missional frontier together. But it's not just you. Maybe you've also got a spouse and some kids. Maybe the people in your huddle are joining in too. As the growing leaders are discipled by a skilled missional leader, they have access to that leader's life, as well as the life of his or her family. *So does the growing leader's family.* What's happened is that a small extended family is starting to form.

So a Huddle of 4-10 becomes an extended group that has 25 people or more once you factor in spouses and kids, even if only one person per nuclear family is actually in the formal Huddle.

The leadership engine is shaping you in missional leadership. But you, your family, and the others in your Huddle are having some powerful experiences along the way. You are slowly but surely moving from consumers to producers, and you are seeing powerful inner transformation. You are seeing the Kingdom come in specific places in your city. People are coming to faith. You are winning battles and losing battles. You are right in the thick of it. Eventually, something starts to *happen* within this group. Eventually, given enough time, the group starts to function like a family.

When a group of people shares experiences like these, going through things that are hard but worth it, it bonds them together far beyond what is usual given the years they've been together. They stop functioning just in relation to the leader and start functioning in relation to each other. So the pipeline stops being an engine and starts being a house.

LEADER
OIKOS

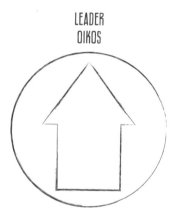

The word the New Testament uses for this is *oikos*. A spiritual family has developed and is now a household of leaders. And soon, these missional leaders will create households of their own as they are sent out to be leaders in their own right.

This is why we don't run a church like we run a business. Ultimately, when the leadership pipeline is working correctly, we should be running a church like we run a family. That's because of the power of *oikos*.

HISTORICAL OIKOS

There is a very important tie between *oikos* (the households of faith of 20-70 we read about in the Bible) and discipleship in the New Testament. You see, in the Gospels and the book of Acts, the word "disciple" is used over and over again. But then, out of nowhere, after the book of Acts that word virtually disappears from scripture. There's no mention of the word "disciple."

It has been argued by some that this means that discipleship is now in the hands of "The Church" and people are spiritually formed almost exclusively through church participation. The concept of one person investing into the life of another, giving his or her own life as something worth imitating, no longer applies.

My belief is that it is still alive and well, but *it was then primarily discussed in the metaphor of parent and child*. In a more Jewish tradition, the premise of having disciples made sense. But in a more Greek culture, the way a parent relates to a child connects more with the audience while still carrying the context of how discipleship happens. So you have Paul calling Timothy his "dear son" and the Apostle John, over and over again, pleading with his "dearly loved children."

The metaphor was that as we raise children to maturity, teaching them invaluable life skills and lessons, we too must have spiritual parents that invest in us, nurture us and lead us to maturity as spiritual children. For the majority of the New Testament, that is the way it discusses discipleship, in the metaphor of parent to child.

And what was the context in which this relationship was nurtured and developed? Through the place and prominence of the *oikos*, the household, the extended family.

To place this point historically, in the third and fourth centuries, the first renewal movements swept through the church through early monastic communities. The first leaders of these communities were called *abba* (daddy/papa/father), whether they were men or women, because it was a genderless expression for the person. It signified they were being parented and "fathered" as God was continuing to father them all.

The point? In the whole of the New Testament and all the way through the early church, discipleship within an extended family context was inseparable. And each extended family had someone leading the family.

PLAY + PURPOSE

Many men can build a fortune but few men can build a family. — J.S. Bryan[35]

A fully functioning oikos develops a texture, a feel, and a visceral quality that everyone senses (whether you're "officially" in it or not), but few can really put a finger on.

But if you take away that dynamic oikos/family texture:

- Morning prayer feels like staff devotion.
- Huddle feels like a stale small group.
- Missional Communities become forced mission projects.

As I've observed the art of creating extended families over the past 35 years, I've noticed that it always takes a combination of two things: **play** and **purpose**.

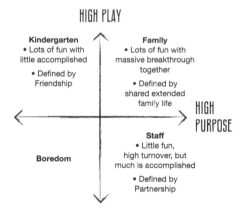

Families play together and have fun, both through planned events and through things that happen organically that you can never plan. But they also have a very clear purpose for why they exist and what God has called them to.

At 3DM, this reality is woven into our team. It happens with the monkey we squeeze around the office when we have an important breakthrough.

....

[35] As quoted from Guy Kawasaki's book *Enchantment: The Art of Changing Hearts, Minds and Actions*

It happens by seeing movies together and having fun together. It happens by going to our kids' plays or soccer games together or through karaoke together. Each of these is just as important as the sermon you give on Sunday or the missional training you give your leaders or the staff/business meeting on Monday mornings.

You plan for play and purpose, but you also cultivate a culture in which it's happening organically. There are some events that serve as a trellis for the growing plant that is your culture, but if that's it, you won't get what you're hoping for.

Here are some questions you might ask about the team you're serving with:

- Would I want to go on vacation with them?
- Would I voluntarily choose to hang out with them and their families because I want to and not because it's forced?
- Am I doing things that let them into the life of me and my family?

Here's the issue: Creating this kind of extended family isn't something you should do because you might find yourself on staff at a church. *It's not your job.* You do this because you're human. Because you need it. Because God created you this way. You do this because you'd want to have this kind of life whether you were paid for it or not. What I'm saying is we should eagerly desire this integrated reality for our own teams.

I wonder, is this the reality in which we find ourselves?

TIPS FOR CREATING YOUR OIKOS

My good friend Keld Dahlmann is leading an amazing missional movement in Scandanavia. He teaches leaders he is shaping these six principles for creating an *oikos*[36]:

1. Shared vision (What do we exist for? In other words, in what way is this community going to bring heaven to earth?)
2. Shared resources

....

[36] Clearly this is a quick snapshot of how to build this kind of extended family experience. See the book *Launching Missional Communities* for much more detail on how to do this.

3. Extended family (This is more than a nuclear family. We'd say a minimum of 15-20 people, a max of 50)
4. Mom/Dad (Leaders in fathering mode)
5. Prayer
6. Common meal

Think about the people you are training to be Missional Leaders. Think about their families connected to them that are now connected to you. What would it look like to create this kind of leader household? What would you need to do?

One issue, of course, is time. Are we just adding more to our already overscheduled lives? My strong word of encouragement is to simply ask people to join in on what you're already doing in the rhythm of your family's life. If you always have dinner at 6 p.m. on Thursdays as a family, simply invite people into that. Don't add something else; have people join in on the good thing that's already happening.

The principle of joining in is a vital one to pass on to your current or future Missional Leaders. Don't work harder — work smarter.

Another thing we found to be quite helpful is authorizing something and giving people permission to call a spade a spade. Here's what I mean. Often, you have a group of people who are regularly coming together because of a common missional activity, and they're starting to affiliate with that community and spend more time with them. On the other hand, you have other groups of people already spending a good amount of time together through affiliation and have started to go out to do missional activity together.

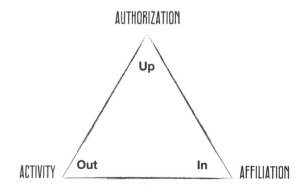

What these people need is for you to call it what it is: A functioning extended family on mission (or Missional Community or whatever terminology you have for it). They just need the authorization that it is what it is. If they are doing UP/IN/OUT together, give it your stamp of approval, authorize it, and simply hold them accountable to pursuing all three dimensions of UP/IN/OUT in that community.

A WORD OF CAUTION

Here is one word of caution for you. You've probably heard these two maxims of leadership before.

- You reproduce who you are.
- Leaders define culture.

These realities are very true, and you need to be aware of their unintended consequences. **If you don't attend to it, your leader oikos will only reproduce *one kind of leader*.**

This goes back to the idea of fivefold ministry and competency. If you're an evangelist, chances are you are going to reproduce and shape your missional leaders to be evangelists. If you're a pastor, you'll shape them to be pastors. If you're a prophet, you'll shape them to be prophets.

Just as spending time in each of the various phases outside of your base is important, it's equally important that you are shaping the missional leaders in your pipeline to be who God created *them to be*, not to be carbon copies of yourself. You may be an evangelist, and they can learn a lot from a phase as an evangelist if they are apostles. But at the end of the day, they need to be an apostle, not an evangelist. As you are training and releasing missional leaders, make sure to keep a steady eye on this.

You need a leadership pipeline that produces all five kinds of missional leaders, not just the kind that you are. Moreover, because leaders define culture, your culture will tend to value whatever you as the leader value. Therefore, it's extraordinarily important you understand and value the need for all of the fivefold ministries.

Here's a helpful way of understanding why this is important:

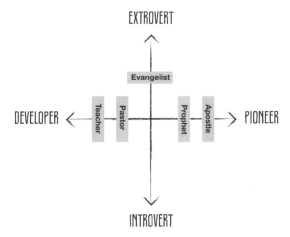

Each of the fivefold ministries represents a place on the continuum from Pioneer to Developer, and so each ministry is massively valuable in terms of mission. Pioneers take ground; developers cultivate ground. If all we have is pioneers who charge forward, taking the rough and undeveloped frontier, we will never keep the land that they've won. There isn't a developer there to make sure the land is developed, maintained, and brought to fruition. All the land is lost.

By the same token, without pioneers, we never get any new territory, and so our communities become stagnant and slip into decline because there isn't any new land to develop.

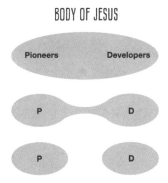

I would argue that almost all church splits usually happen because there is unresolved conflict happening between Pioneers and Developers. They haven't figured out how to work together and they haven't figured out why they need each other.

About 70 percent of the population are developers and 30 percent are pioneers. *We've got to have both working together.* It's important to recognize that whenever we engage in a missional conversation, it's usually going to attract pioneers. Let's be careful to make sure we are going slow enough to take along the developers who will cultivate land once we get there, while still pushing the pace so we make it to the frontier.

This is the goal behind the leadership pipeline — recruiting the right people and then training them, deploying them into mission, and reviewing what happens. As we do this, the leadership engine will move them from D1 to D4, and we will begin to see a spiritual family emerge.

As we do this, we will need to help our leaders with paradigm shifts and practical realities. The next chapter uncovers a key aspect of each.

7

∾ COVENANTS + CAPITALS ∾

After working with leaders over the past 30 years, I have discovered the importance of two distinct things that have helped me shape cultures where leaders can be empowered and released for Kingdom success. One is a paradigm; the other is a practical reality. I want to take a chapter to share these thoughts with you, because I believe it will help missional leaders in your *oikos* as much as it has helped missional leaders in mine.

PARADIGM SHIFT — COVENANTS

Missional leaders will need to embrace a more Kingdom-oriented understanding of how God says our world functions, both in terms of why we're here in the world and more specifically, in terms of how we make decisions. I believe that scripture lays out a proper ordering of our priorities:

1. Our covenant with God, our Father

2. Our covenant with our spouse and kids

3. Our missional calling and family: Where and to whom am I *currently* called?

4. Our job

I don't think this is a revolutionary list until we get to the third point. That's because in this list I am suggesting that a person's calling to missional leadership should *dictate* the type of job that person has and where it's located.

I cannot count the number of people over the years who have felt called to our community and to a specific missional endeavor in that place but chose to leave the city and move for an annual pay increase of $5,000 or $10,000. Let's be very clear about what they said when making that decision: "Five to ten grand a year is worth more than the missional calling God has placed on my life and the family I was serving with."

That is, quite literally, what their life is saying.

I've seen more pastors than I can count make that exact same decision. When we do this, we are using the values and the metrics that the world considers important to dictate our decisions instead of Kingdom realities. The Kingdom reality is that we have a Father who says, "Look at the birds in the air. I take care of them. Won't I take care of you?"[37]

Look. I'm not suggesting we work for ridiculously small amounts of money to the point where we can't take care of our family. That would violate our covenant with our spouse and kids, which is a rung above our specific missional calling. But I am saying that time and time again, people make decisions based on money, stuff, opportunity, glamour, celebrity, consumerism, or ambition *rather than asking where God is calling them to go*. Missional leaders simply have a different way of making decisions, and so you would be wise to shape this Kingdom reality in the missional leaders you are training.

Let's look at a practical example. Let's say one of the missional leaders in your Huddle is offered a promotion for more money. Awesome. That's great. Anyone's knee-jerk reaction would be, "Take it! Take the money and the promotion and keep moving up the corporate ladder."

But these would be questions I'd want to ask this missional leader:

- If you take this job, will you be able to be faithful to your covenant with God? Will you still have time to spend with him? Will you still be in a place where you work from rest, rather than rest from work?

- How will taking this job affect your family? Will it bring more stress? Will you still get quality time with your spouse and your kids? Will you still have time for family activities that you do together?

....

[37] Matthew 6:26

- Will you still have the availability to serve the people you feel God is calling you to serve? What would change? Are you still being called to serve these people?

- Is the increase in money and stature worth whatever decreases may come with it?

What we are doing in situations like this is helping the missional leaders we are training to live with a Kingdom understanding of how we order our lives and make decisions. We don't answer to money. We don't answer to stuff. We don't answer to ambition, and we aren't slaves to our appetites. We answer to God.

My friend Todd Hunter puts it this way: "You are an agent of the Kingdom cleverly disguised as an attorney (or artist, or banker, or mom, or electrician, etc).["][38]

I believe this is a crucial area to address for all missional leaders, because it's one of those subtle things that our enemy uses to dull our effectiveness. Seriously, how brilliant is this? He sees that someone is starting to get some missional traction, and so he gets him or her a $7,000 raise across the country that takes him or her out of the game for a couple of years. We have to see that this is happening all around us and help our leaders see this reality.

PRACTICAL REALITY — FIVE CAPITALS

The second thing to explore is a practical reality that you'll need to come to grips with if you want to shape and multiply missional leaders.

Luke shares a fascinating story that Jesus told. It's a parable about a shrewd manager, and most of us don't quite know what to do with it.

> [1]Jesus told his disciples: "There was a rich man whose manager was accused of wasting his possessions. [2]So he called him in and asked him, 'What is this I hear about you? Give an account of your management, because you cannot be manager any longer.'

....

[38] This quote was taken from Todd Hunter at the 2010 Ecclesia National Gathering

³"The manager said to himself, 'What shall I do now? My master is taking away my job. I'm not strong enough to dig, and I'm ashamed to beg — ⁴I know what I'll do so that, when I lose my job here, people will welcome me into their houses.'

⁵"So he called in each one of his master's debtors. He asked the first, 'How much do you owe my master?'

⁶"'Nine hundred gallons of olive oil,' he replied.

"The manager told him, 'Take your bill, sit down quickly, and make it four hundred and fifty.'

⁷Then he asked the second, 'And how much do you owe?'

"'A thousand bushels of wheat,' he replied.

"He told him, 'Take your bill and make it eight hundred.'

⁸"The master commended the dishonest manager because he had acted shrewdly. For the people of this world are more shrewd in dealing with their own kind than are the people of the light. ⁹I tell you, use worldly wealth to gain friends for yourselves, so that when it is gone, you will be welcomed into eternal dwellings."³⁹

Let me suggest to you what I think all of this is about. I've spent time talking to economists about this and obviously economists look at the world through the lens of capital. Of course, Karl Marx coined that phrase in relation to a broader spectrum of reality than just money when he wrote *Das Kapital*. He recognized the practical reality that the way the world works is with a series of relationships in which particular capital is invested in particular ways.

For example, you'll hear economists talk about social capital. Some of them will speak of the infrastructure around us as the infrastructure capital of a place or town. They come to a location and are able to audit that location based on the quality of the roads, lampposts, the planting of trees, landscaping, and much more. It's all capital.

Now what I've noticed is this: You can line up economists so they go head to toe all around the world, and they still won't agree with everything because economics is something where everyone has their own opinion. Here, I'm going to offer my opinion, and it may very well be wrong. But obviously, I

....

³⁹ Luke 16

wouldn't be sharing it with you if I thought otherwise. That's why it's called an opinion.

I think there are five capitals we see in scripture that are also all around the world we live in.

1. **Spiritual:** How much faith do you have to invest?
2. **Relational:** How much relational equity do you have to invest?
3. **Physical:** How much time and energy do you have to invest?
4. **Intellectual:** What intellect, skill sets, and competencies do you have to invest?
5. **Financial**: How much financial capital do you have to invest?[40]

This list is ordered from the hardest to get (Spiritual) to the easiest to get (Financial).

Here's the interesting thing. In the world and even in the church, this list is reversed. Think about the rich young man who went away sad because he had such wealth. This is what Jesus was saying: The way you view capital in your life is completely backward. Jesus was saying that a relationship with him and a relationship with the Father, living in their Kingdom, was the pearl of great price. That was one economic metaphor used. Here's another: A treasure in a field.

What you need to do, says Jesus, is this: "Sell everything! Give up everything, cash it all in for the one thing that's more important than everything else."[41]

So spiritual capital is way more important than all of the other forms of capital.

What is Jesus saying in Luke 16 with the shrewd (and slightly dishonest!) manager? To me, it is this: Relational capital is more important and harder to find than financial capital — so use your money to buy friends! That's the punchline of the parable. It's not like there is another one! Jesus was telling us to invest our money into people's lives, and maybe we'll get friendship out of it. In other words, recognize where each kind of capital is in its ordering.

....

[40] We can think of social capital, which we discussed earlier, simply as a combination of the middle three.

[41] Matthew 13:44

The reason Jesus praised the shrewd manager is that he was smart enough to know how the world worked and how to trade on the capitals at his disposal. He knew very soon he was going to need a job because he was about to be fired. Do you know what's good to have when you don't have a job? Friends who can help you get a job! Jesus wasn't praising the man for being lazy or conniving but simply for understanding how the trading of capitals work. And clearly Jesus was asking us to see how they work.

So how do you make a missional leader?

You make a missional leader by investing *all five capitals* into that person. You're going to need all five. All of them are necessary to make just one. All of the capitals are the sum total of your life, and if you want to make another one of you that the Spirit is at work in, you've got to invest everything you have.

The issue is that your capitals may be in a rather unhelpful or unusual order. For instance, you might have intellectual capital much higher on your list, because in the Western church, we value intellectual capital more than most anything else. How do I know this? Churches usually hire pastors based on three things:

1. How well they preach (Intellectual capital)
2. How organizationally gifted they are (Intellectual capital)
3. How well they can raise money (Financial capital because it is based on a person's ability to increase that specific capital.)

Let's be brutally honest and admit this is why people are hired in the Western church. But this isn't the way things should be!

I want to make sure I'm very clear in explaining how these capitals work. First, they are in descending order. Even more, each capital is also something like 10 times more important than the one beneath it. Physical capital is so much more important than intellectual capital. How do I know that? Because if I have a migraine headache, I can't read a book. If I have a killer toothache, I can't go to work. I mean, it's only one tooth, but it's excruciatingly painful. Intellectual capital doesn't work if you're sick. It doesn't work if you're burnt out, exhausted, or on the verge of a nervous breakdown.

Most of us have put financial and intellectual capital ahead of physical. If you haven't, you're a very unusual person. But most of your congregation, in terms of the way they spend most of their weeks, are doing precisely that. They are putting money ahead of their health all the time, aren't they?

Quite honestly, when you see the way that churches run, we've fallen in line with Western consumerism and its view of value rather than the way that Jesus describes his value of capital.

Let's think about relational capital. Do you genuinely believe that relational capital is 10 times more important than physical capital? I definitely do. I believe that of all the five capitals, relational falls just under spiritual capital. I believe this because Jesus' last words to you and me were that he wanted us to make disciples. The most important capital involved in making disciples is spiritual and relational, because you can't make a disciple without relationship, and you can't make a disciple without God's help.

The interesting thing is that we create our lives and build our lives without much reference to relational capital. So friendships suffer. Families suffer. Marriages suffer. Why? Because one of the lower capitals is higher up than it's meant to be. Many evangelical Christians in North America might put spiritual capital first, but they'd put financial right under it, wouldn't they? They might not say that, but that's the way they act, and it shows what they believe.

Parents are working so hard to earn money to provide their kids with the best stuff that they've become absentee parents, allowing screens of various types (TV, computer, iPad) to raise them. Then, they wonder why their kids aren't disciples. You can't disciple your kids if you aren't in front of them!

People sometimes ask me about my kids: "Your kids seem to be alright. What did you do?"

What did we do? We had breakfast and dinner together every single day.

"What about when you had something early in the morning?"

Then we all got up early.

"What if you had something late?"

Then we had a late dinner. Maybe the kids need to be fed most of dinner, but at least we could do dessert together. We had breakfast and dinner together.

"What about when you traveled, because you traveled a lot, right?"

Well, we had daddy's breakfast every week, and the kids got to decide where they were taking their dad for breakfast on a Saturday morning. When they were little it was always McDonalds. They *loved* McDonalds. It was like Shangri-la to them.

But by the time they were old and sophisticated, they wanted to go to Cafe Rouge. So when Beccy got older, we'd go there and eat our scrambled eggs and read our newspapers. Right before Beccy was married, do you know what she said to me?

"Can we do a daddy's breakfast just one more time?"

I'm just like everyone else. I accidentally dropped the kids on their heads. I thought they'd break at any minute. I have no idea how to put on a diaper. I could barely put clothes on them. You only get good at it afterward! But what that moment told me is that at least I got some of it in the right order.
The physical capital that we offer people is our time and our energy. If you don't have any time for people, I can guarantee you won't be able to make a relationship with them.

Now here's an interesting twist: You can invest capital for a return, and you can invest it for somebody else. Let me give you an example. Sally and I had been coming to Pawleys Island, South Carolina, for more than a decade. We'd bring pastors on retreat and often speak at the local church in the summers. In return, the church would give us a vacation house on the beach, which was fantastic. We had been coming here year after year. We'd show up, and I'd teach a few times in the summer, but I quite frankly had no idea if this really meant anything or not. But when we moved to Pawleys Island permanently to start 3DM, people started coming out of the woodwork.

The families who came with Sally and me, the team we were forming, didn't know anything or anybody when they arrived. But they got to trade on my capital. They got a head start. You know that's true, don't you? If you invite someone into a relationship with one of your previously existing friends, that new person benefits from the relational capital you've already invested.

What I want to say is this: When you think about making a missional leader, you have to get out of the box-checking mentality. You have to stop thinking about discipleship as the one hour a week in your Huddle, because you don't make disciples that way. You need that time, but you need a lot of other things too.

If you want to make a missional leader, it's going to take everything you've got. Not what the church has; what *you* have. Your spiritual life. Your relationships. Your time and energy. Your skill sets and gifts. Your money. It's going to take all of it just to produce one missional leader.

And as Jesus said, you will receive a disproportionate return on the investment. This is the reality of investing capital shrewdly.

8

CREATING A CULTURE OF
◟ SHARED LEADERSHIP ◞

If you're going to create a community where leaders can flourish, you're going to have to create a certain kind of culture. It's the only way that can happen. And whenever you talk about creating culture, you've got to start with language. You may have heard the saying that "language creates culture," and it's true. What you say, how you say it, and the mediums you use to say it will create a certain kind of culture.

The problem for most of us is that we have a language people are using, but it's by accident. As a result, the language is not creating the culture we want. But it doesn't have to be that way. We need to approach culture-making with serious intentionality, allowing a shared language and vocabulary to create the culture God is calling us to shape.

To create the type of leadership culture we are talking about, you will need more than the discipling language we first introduced in *Building a Discipling Culture* that we talked about in Chapter 6. You will need a language — or what we call a Vocab — that no one but your community can create. It must express the very essence of who you are and what God is calling you to do.

The specific Vocab that will create your leadership culture will be determined by your:
- Vision
- Values
- Valuation
- Vehicles

Let's break down each of these four things in more detail.

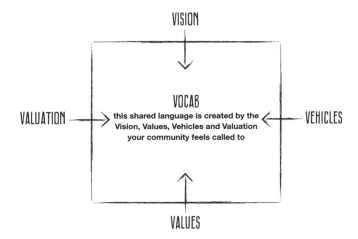

VISION

Most churches have a vision statement that they have probably done a lot of work on. Think about your vision statement. With that vision statement in mind, I would ask you this question: Does the vision for your team, your church, or your life articulate the Kingdom in any clear way? If your vision doesn't express the Kingdom, I would say it is more of a mission statement.

Mission statements are great. They usually say what you are going to do with your vision. But I believe vision should be an expression of the Kingdom, a reality that that we long to be fully expressed. The Kingdom has been inaugurated and consummated in Jesus, but we long for its fulfillment.
What does this fulfillment look like? Thankfully, we see it in the life of Jesus. In Jesus we see the life of the Kingdom being portrayed here on earth.

As Jesus was being baptized, heaven was opened. The Holy Spirit remained upon him permanently, serving as a permanent link between heaven and earth in Jesus. Everything present in heaven is now available on earth in Jesus. That is the point of the gospels, so that:

> In heaven there is no sin; in Jesus there is forgiveness.
>
> In heaven there is no sickness; in Jesus there is healing.
>
> In heaven there is no Satan; in Jesus there is deliverance.

In heaven there is no sadness; in Jesus we find joy.

In heaven there is no strife; in Jesus we find peace.

Jesus is the portal to the future that we long for. When we come to Jesus, we touch the future. When Jesus reaches out and touches us, the future touches our lives.

The Kingdom has come. Jesus said, "If I cast out demons by the finger of God, then the Kingdom is among you."[42] Jesus made it very clear that the Kingdom of God is going to be a battle, because the reality of the Kingdom is a declaration of war against the occupying power of the Devil, who is the prince of this world. Jesus came to overthrow this occupying power by declaring and demonstrating that there is a kingdom more powerful than the one that occupies the world right now. Our vision is of that coming Kingdom.

This is what we are looking for. If it's your vision, it should be your vision **statement**. There should be something in that statement that is a declaration of the good news of the Kingdom that is being inaugurated through your community.

Our vision in Sheffield was about calling a city back to God. The church is in the city to bring the Kingdom, and if the Kingdom is being brought to the city through the church, then we are going to call the people back to God. It was very simple.

Here's the thing: When you have a big enough vision, you can get everyone underneath it. Let's think about this in terms of a Missional Community. In Sheffield, every Missional Community is fulfilling the vision of the church calling a city back to God, even though one community is working among the prostitutes, one among wealthy professionals, and another one among children of families. All of them get to fulfill the big vision with their own vision.

If you are going to have a successful launch of lots and lots of Missional Communities, every leader has to have his or her own vision, and each leader's vision has to align with the big vision.

Think of it this way: If your leadership pipeline is functioning the way I have

---

[42] Luke 11:20

described, eventually, over time, it's going to produce someone who is able to lead their own missional family. That's what we're trying to produce — a leader who can lead his or her own family.

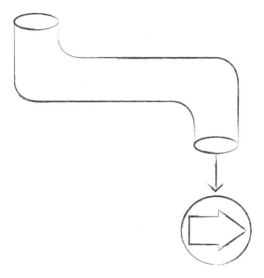

If you have a vision that's big enough, you can have hundreds and hundreds of leaders working together, going after the same vision while each owning their own vision that God has called them to. Today, there are more than 300 Missional Communities in Sheffield. And they are just getting started.

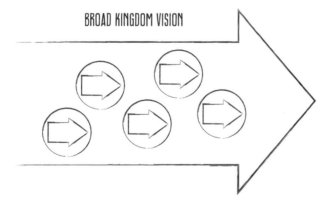

BROAD KINGDOM VISION

VALUES

Vision is about Kingdom, and values are about relationships. Vision is the call of a community to represent God and his coming Kingdom. Our values are about covenant, the call to a relationship of oneness with God and with each other.

Here's the question we want to grapple with when thinking about values: If God our Father were fully present, what would the relationships in our community consist of?

Now we are not coming up with an abstract series of statements that are the values of your church. That can be a waste of time if the statements aren't based in reality. Values should come out of the life of the church that you are leading. They need to be based on what is real. Your values should reflect *what is already present, not what you are hoping will one day be present*. What are the values we're already living out that are specifically for this community of people?

An example might be helpful. When I first become the senior leader of St. Thomas, our church was tangentially a part of a pretty significant scandal. A service that once met in our church and had since launched to do its own thing had become grossly immoral. It was a nightmare. Because we were the only church in any way attached to it, all the press came down on our church. I became the leader in the midst of that firestorm.

Quickly, accountability became a paramount value for us. So we increased the level of accountability in many different ways at St. Thomas. This eventually led to the creation of the discipleship vehicle now called Huddle. Our vocab created a certain kind of culture because we had a value *and* a vehicle to deliver that value. We embraced a radical Matthew 18:15 culture that said if anyone has wronged you, you go straight to that person and to no one else. Don't gossip with your friends. Don't come complaining to the pastor. Go. To. Them.[43]

The results were startling. In the 10 years that I was the pastor of one of the fastest growing churches in Europe, there was not one divorce among the 700-800 couples we married. To this day, 17 years later, there have only been two. That sounds like a covenant community, doesn't it? This is what can happen when a value is truly worked out in a community and you have a vehicle to actively accomplish that working out.

Those are numbers worth counting, right?

....

[43] Matthew 18:15: "If your brother or sister sins, go and point out their fault, just between the two of you. If they listen to you, you have won them over."

Speaking of counting . . .

VALUATION

As we move to valuation, there is a principle at work: You count what you value and you value what you count. This is what valuation does — count the right things. The real issue is that most of us are not counting the things that Jesus is counting. For far too long, most of our churches have primarily counted the ABCs —attendance, buildings, and cash. The issue, of course, is that this isn't what Jesus counted.

Jesus counted disciples. Not people who just showed up. Not people who were nice. Not people who tossed a few dollars his way. He counted disciples.

Remember, a disciple is someone who has the character of Jesus and the competency of Jesus. It's about faithfulness and fruit. The problem, of course, is figuring out how to measure those things. We should be measuring things. We should be evaluating what is happening in the life of our community. But we need to make sure we are counting the right things.

So as we talk about faithfulness and fruit, what we are really talking about is **quality** and **quantity**.

You can't really measure faithfulness, can you? It's more of a qualitative thing. Since you can't measure faithfulness by numbers, you have to measure it by something else. Do the lives of the people in your community more and more resemble the character of Jesus? Are people able to hear the voice of God and respond? Do they tell the truth? Do they do the right thing when no one is looking? Do they take bold steps of faith? Are they becoming more mature?

You can't really quantitatively measure that, but it's still important to figure out how your community will evaluate the quality of spiritual life the people in your community are living.

All that being said, you can measure fruit. You can count that. You can count how many apples a tree produces. The real question, then, is what you are calling fruit. What are the things that your community will count as fruit that you honestly believe Jesus would count?

I'll clue you in: While your attendance says *something* about your church, I'm not sure it ever really says the thing we're looking for. Kingdom fruit always follows faithfulness. There are times when we feel like God is calling our community to do something, and it means we lose people as the attendance goes down. But we were faithful. If we were only counting attendance, we would miss out on counting what matters most to God.

Should you count money? Sure. A church will have bills to pay. But will you judge your success or failure based on that? How much will you talk about money? How often will it work its way into your language?

People will know what you care about by what you count and how you communicate it. What will your community count so that missional leaders know what they are really going after?

VEHICLES

What are the vehicles that are going to deliver your vision, your values, and your valuation through the vocab that your community has agreed on?

Back in the 1960s there was a communication genius named Marshall McLuhan whom very few people knew about. He has since passed away, but he is now considered one of the most respected thinkers of the twentieth century. This was his most famous principle: *The medium is the message.* In other words, the vehicle that you use to deliver your message actually shapes *what the message is*.

We'll use an extreme example to bring this insight to light. Let's say you've been dating someone for quite some time and you decide you wanted to ask him or her to marry you. You know you want to spend the rest of your life with this person, to start a family with him or her, and to do mission with him or her. This is the person for you. That's some serious commitment we're talking about and some serious feelings you are trying to express.

Now imagine trying to express those feelings and making that proposal via a text message.

Somehow, you could say the *exact same thing* you would say if you were sitting across the table, and yet the message will somehow lose something because of the vehicle the message used.

This is what we need to consider when we are using a shared vocabulary to express our vision, values, and valuation. Do we have vehicles that *incarnate* what we are expressing? If we don't, I promise that message won't be delivered like you hope. Can you imagine me saying accountability was a value for St. Thomas if there was no vehicle to practice accountability?

Think about your vision, your values, and your valuation. Think about what the Lord is calling you to do. Now think about the corporate practices that your community finds life in. Here are a few vehicles we have used in churches I've been a part of. (Some will sound familiar by now.)

- **Worship service.** This is a place where the whole body (at least 75 people) gathers, worships, takes the Lord's Supper, submits to the teaching of the word, hears stories of triumph, lives into a bigger story, and casts broad vision.

- **Huddles.** A discipleship and training vehicle for 4-10 current or future missional leaders through which leaders come to embody the character and competency of Jesus. This allows the church to operate and live with the principle of low control and high accountability.

- **Missional Communities.** A group of 20-50 people on mission together who are called to serve a particular network of people or neighborhood and incarnate the Gospel of Jesus in that context. It often has small groups with the larger community.

- **Small Groups.** A place of community for a group of 6-12 people where there is a strong emphasis on life together and spiritual conversation. It is usually part of several small groups in the same Missional Community, which makes the small-group experience far more potent.

- **Learning Community.** A training and reflection vehicle for Missional Community leaders that happens every 6-9 months. This is a place for missional leaders to gather, reflect on where their groups are, hear fresh vision from the Lord, and plan for the future in the context of other MC leaders. The most successful Learning Communities for missional leaders are often a collection of several churches in the same geographic region.

In many of the churches we work with, here is how some of these Vehicles work together when we look at it from a sociological perspective of the four different space people inhabit.[44]

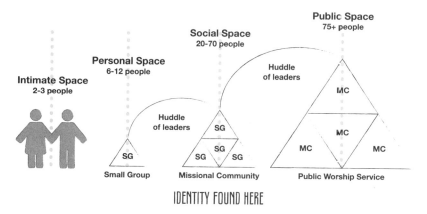

Public Space
75+ people

Social Space
20-70 people

Personal Space
6-12 people

Intimate Space
2-3 people

Huddle of leaders

MC

Huddle of leaders

SG

SG

MC

SG

SG

SG

MC

MC

Small Group

Missional Community

Public Worship Service

IDENTITY FOUND HERE

It's important we don't assume that we've discovered all of the missional or discipling vehicles already. God is constantly doing new work in different places that we can learn from. Recently one of the missionaries we sent from St. Thomas to South Africa found a new vehicle called *Discovery Groups* that was first pioneered in Asia. Jenny has been working among the poorest of the poor, not even in the townships, but in the actual ghettos beyond the townships. These ghettos are basically groups of rootless people.

With Discovery Groups, all you do is look for Persons of Peace (people God has already prepared in advance to be open to you and the mission he has put on your heart) and simply ask, "Would you like to discover more about God?"

If the person says yes, Jenny says, "You would? GREAT. I'll train you to do it. I won't do any teaching or preaching. You'll do it with your group. I'll come to your household."

They gather at the household, read a passage, and ask themselves what the passage means. Then they ask, "What am I going to do about it?" The level of transformation and Kingdom breakthrough that she is seeing in these people's lives is absolutely incredible!

....

[44] Sociological understanding of "spaces" Taken from the E.T. Hall study from the 1960's on Proxemics. For a fuller understanding of this, see my book *Launching Missional Communities: A Field Guide*

THE CART AND THE HORSE

Here's the key for every vehicle you use: It needs to be lightweight and low maintenance. If the majority of these vehicles are going to be run by missional leaders who aren't getting paid and who have full-time jobs and families, they need to be relatively easy to run and maintain and light enough to move quickly.

As you are evaluating the vehicles you currently have, here are two questions to ask:

1. What percentage of our annual budget is going to this particular vehicle? (This could be in terms of upkeep, staff, facilities, or other factors.)

2. What percentage of staff time is going toward maintaining this particular vehicle?

These questions will reveal what you value, how you hope to deliver your vision, and which vehicles are most important to you. Chances are that your worship service is most important — it likely is the vehicle that is getting most of your time and money and the vehicle where you are expecting most things to happen. (This is likely the case whether you want to admit it or not.)

I'm not one of those people who feel that the worship service isn't important. I think worship services are incredibly important. But there are certain things the worship service is for and certain things it isn't for.

My guess would be that between 60 and 90 percent of your church's time and budget is spent in some way, shape, or form around those Sunday morning activities. This is the case in most churches. Well, if you want to release a host of missional leaders to be on the front lines of mission, you need to address this.

Let's be clear: I'm not suggesting that you change everything over night. I'm always going to suggest *evolution* rather than *revolution*. Revolutions are bloody and expensive, and usually everyone ends up dead.

So what do you do? Imagine that your church is a cart and a horse. There are things in your church that are higher maintenance, that require a lot of organization. This is fine up to a point. But the horse — the thing that pulls the cart — is your missional leaders. They are the ones who are going to lead the church onto the missional frontier and take the cart with them. The problem comes when we have carts that are too heavy and ornate, too inflexible and high maintenance. If that is the case, the cart will end up pulling the horse instead of the other way around. And while that's certainly a comical situation, it's not one you want to have to fix.

If you're in this situation, this is what you need to do: Feed the horse and slowly make the cart more lightweight and low maintenance. That's the key.

Here's one example: If you're someone who teaches or preaches regularly and you're spending 30 hours a week on the message, discipline yourself to do it in 20 hours. How might you use an additional 10 hours that week to invest in the lives of your missional leaders? What if time spent in creative meetings were cut back by 25 percent? What if money usually allocated for Sunday mornings were cut back by a certain percentage and re-allocated? These are just a few of the dozens of things you could do to lighten the cart.

One of the others things we've discovered works is something called *studied neglect*. Many leaders out there are more prone to revolution, and instead of being patient with this process, they take a sledgehammer to the cart rather than the scalpel that is needed. What they'll do is kill off all programs, events, and vehicles they deem as too heavyweight and high maintenance in one fell swoop. Please don't do that! We've found studied neglect is a much easier way. It's a pretty easy thing: Rather than killing anything, simply stop resourcing it.

Why? Because you want to resource the places where there is Kingdom breakthrough. Any time resources are going somewhere else, it's taking away from the breakthrough. This sounds counter-intuitive, but it's true. You don't send more resources to where you're losing; you send resources to where you're winning. That's where you invest your money and energy and time and everything else.

Think of it terms of a war. You don't need to win every battle to win the war. In fact, most of the time, you only need one offensive breakthrough where you penetrate enemy lines to suddenly arrive in the heart of the enemy's territory. In effect, that is what the Allied forces did on the beaches of Normandy. They put all of their resources into that one battle and made sure they won it. They knew that if they won there, they would have a beachhead that would carry them straight to Berlin.

So don't kill the programs or events or fight battles you don't have to. Just don't resource them. Put the resources where you see breakthrough on the horizon.

Lastly, know that if you're thinking about really going after multiplying missional leaders, there are things you're currently doing that you're going to need to stop. Jim Collins pointed out so wonderfully in his book *Good to Great* that the organizations that consistently went from being good to being great were disciplined about starting and stopping. Whenever they started something new, they made sure they were stopping at least as much as they were starting. When this happened, the organizations hit an inflection because more of their resources were going to a place of breakthrough.

You have a finite amount of time. Energy. Resources. Attention. Whenever you start something, you are taking something from that limited pool.

What will you stop?

So here is quick a summary:
- Feed the horse. Slowly make the cart more lightweight and low maintenance.
- Resource the places where there is breakthrough using studied neglect.
- Whenever you start something, stop something.

If you do these things in the community you lead, you will create the space and the discipline needed to multiply missional leaders. What we see is that when leaders are trained well and released, when they are given more than a 10'x10' playground to operate in, they can all function extraordinarily well together. They stop being competitive with each other and start competing against our common enemy.

That is the power of a missional movement.

And chances are, God is calling you to start one.

RENEWAL, EXOSKELETONS, ✑ + DESOLATE WASTELAND ✑

We have seen in this book how to multiply missional leaders. By focusing on character and competency (and specifically competency in all of the fivefold ministries), by finding the right people to recruit into the leadership pipeline and then using the leadership engine to develop each of them as individuals, and by creating a vocab of vision within our communities, we can develop missional leaders who can develop missional leaders.

This is a great calling. To fulfill it, we will have to reform and redirect both our lives and the lives of others. To see how we can do this, let's turn to the book of Ezekiel.

> [1]The hand of the LORD was upon me, and he brought me out in the Spirit of the LORD and set me down in the middle of the valley; it was full of bones. [2]And he led me around among them, and behold, there were very many on the surface of the valley, and behold, they were very dry. [3]And he said to me, "Son of man, can these bones live?" And I answered, "O Lord GOD, you know." [4]Then he said to me, "Prophesy over these bones, and say to them, O dry bones, hear the word of the LORD. [5]Thus says the Lord GOD to these bones: Behold, I will cause breath to enter you, and you shall live. [6]And I will lay sinews upon you, and will cause flesh to come upon you, and cover you with skin, and put breath in you, and you shall live, and you shall know that I am the LORD."
>
> [7]So I prophesied as I was commanded. And as I prophesied, there was a sound, and behold, a rattling, and the bones came together, bone to its bone. [8]And I looked, and behold, there were sinews on them, and flesh had come upon them, and skin had covered them. But there was no breath in them. [9]Then he said to me, "Prophesy to the breath; prophesy,

son of man, and say to the breath. Thus says the Lord GOD: Come from the four winds, O breath, and breathe on these slain, that they may live." [10]So I prophesied as he commanded me, and the breath came into them, and they lived and stood on their feet, an exceedingly great army.

[11]Then he said to me, "Son of man, these bones are the whole house of Israel. Behold, they say, 'Our bones are dried up, and our hope is lost; we are indeed cut off.' [12]Therefore prophesy, and say to them. Thus says the Lord GOD: Behold, I will open your graves and raise you from your graves, O my people. And I will bring you into the land of Israel. [13]And you shall know that I am the LORD, when I open your graves, and raise you from your graves, O my people. [14]And I will put my Spirit within you, and you shall live, and I will place you in your own land. Then you shall know that I am the LORD; I have spoken, and I will do it, declares the LORD."[45]

RENEWING

This prophecy, which the Holy Spirit gave Ezekiel, directly applies to our reality as we are called to lead God's people. As leaders of God's people, we are called to be partners with the Lord in what he wants to do. He wants to bring life to his people to renew them. He wants to connect his people and reform them so that they have coherence and connectedness that allows them to stand up. Through his renewing Spirit and reforming work, the Lord wants to redirect his people so he can use them for the purpose he has established. Scripture describes this as the formation of an army, which is a great picture for those of us moving toward the missional frontier.

As I interact with pastors around the world, it's interesting to me how many people desire the renewing of God's Spirit in their community. Many talk about a desire for more Spirit-led worship, passionate prayer, and greater amounts of God's power. You may have similar prayers for your church too, like Ezekiel, see God's Spirit breathed into the bodies and bones of your congregation.

Now, some might believe that the renewal, reforming, and redirecting of a community just happens randomly, almost like magic. You might hear someone espouse this belief by saying that the Spirit moves as it pleases.

....

[45] Ezekiel 37

This is largely true, because God can do what he wants where he wants when he wants. But if we are seeking him, if we are open and available, there is space for God to move among us.

How do we do this? Thankfully, there seem to be some straightforward, logical reasons for a Spiritual outpouring, and there are skills, abilities, and gifts we can acquire. God is a God of order, and he wants to pour out his Spirit on his people. We must get away from the idea that renewal is all smoke and mirrors and that we can't do what churches that experience revival are doing.

Clearly God is in control and we can't manipulate the wind that is his Spirit, but certainly we can raise the sails in readiness, can't we?

So the first thing we do is desire to grow. One of the best ways we can do this is by finding leaders who are ahead of us on the journey and spending time with them and their churches, watching, modeling, asking questions, and then imitating and putting into practice all that we learn *before* we think about innovating.

I remember a time in Sheffield when I felt the Lord really wanted us to enter into a fervent season of prayer, but I realized I wasn't as skilled in leading a community in that. However, I heard of a pastor in Africa who was doing this in amazing ways. So I went for a period of time and sat at his feet, soaking in everything I could, watching, observing, imitating, and doing everything I could. This was a man of God that I felt confident I could learn from. When I went back to Sheffield, while we innovated on this in our own context, the learning came with me. We should always be willing to learn more from people ahead of us on the journey.

REFORMING

As we reflect on the Ezekiel passage, we see the bones start to form to the body by attaching themselves through the tendons and ligaments. This attaching begins through the creation of connective tissue. As we have discussed throughout this book, Huddles are the vehicle that serves as the connective tissue that intentionally joins people together. Intentional discipling relationships are often the means by which God works the reforming process within a congregation. This makes sense given Jesus' model and his command for us to go make disciples.

Over and over again you'll see that as you begin to intentionally disciple missional leaders, something begins to happen within this small portion of your congregation. It feels as though the body is aligning with the principles and the priorities of Jesus. That's because your Huddle *is* aligned with Jesus' first priority to make disciples. Then, surprising and unexpectedly, impossible tasks become possible as Huddles multiply themselves through God's Spirit. Communication becomes easier, reproduction happens on its own, leaders are discovered and recruited, people find their mission, and new life springs up.

Let me give you an example of what aligning the body through the connective tissue of Huddles can look like. On the day of September 11, 2001, the day the Twin Towers fell in America, I was living in England. When the tragic events happened, it was in the middle of our day. I returned from lunch with the bishop to see on television the scenes that we all now have etched into our memories. After just a few moments of watching, I realized we needed to get the leaders of the church together to pray. I called the people in my Huddle and said: "Let's meet in 30 minutes at the church to pray for these horrible attacks. Phone the people in your Huddle, and have them phone their guys, and we'll gather together." Then, I had a cup of tea to settle my nerves, which is what all good English people do when things seem overwhelming. I left my house and walked around the block to the church where, to my amazement, more than 300 leaders were waiting to pray.

It would be next to impossible for most churches to make something like that happen. Most would have to make 250 phone calls or so to do this and even then, attendance would probably be spotty at best. On the other hand, I made maybe six or seven phone calls, and 300 leaders showed up within 30 minutes. In this instance, you can see that the connective tissue was there. The tendons of discipling relationships were pulling the body together and aligning it.

To take the metaphor a step further, I would say that the leadership of a church is the skeleton of the body of Christ. I say this because the skeleton serves as the infrastructure for the church body as a whole. The connective tissue is the discipling relationships, and through those relationships the leaders of the church align the whole body as they work together.

ENDOSKELETONS VS. EXOSKELETONS VS. BLOBS

The world of anatomy identifies two types of skeletons. Endoskeletons, which humans have, are on the inside of the body. Exoskeletons, which we see on grasshoppers or crustaceans, are on the outside of the body. Ezekiel is talking about an endoskeleton in this passage. However, most churches operate as an exoskeleton, not an endoskeleton.

Here's what I mean.

The leadership of a church provides the skeleton that causes the body as a whole to stand up and do the things it's supposed to do. However, it is quite detrimental if the skeleton of leadership is the first thing people *see* about a church. But this happens far too often. Why? Because a high-control church has taken the fear of an unaccountable body to the extreme and as a result, the leadership feels to the need to control everything. Because of that, newcomers encounter leaders as the representatives of the body at everything, all the time. Leaders greet you when you arrive, teach the classes, officiate the services, send you on your way out, and establish the norm for the body in every other way. But because the leader isn't a normal member of the body, encountering a leader first makes someone feel as though a church is extremely difficult to get into.

That's because the person is encountering a shell, an exoskeleton. When leaders create a high-control environment and run essentially all aspects of the church, it inadvertently creates a high bar of commitment and expectation for someone encountering it for the first time. That bar is generally too high, and so the newcomer continues church-shopping or just gives up altogether. On the other hand, if the same newcomer met ordinary, soft tissue, community Christians, it would feel much better. The newcomer would feel like, "Wow, these people are just like me! I think I could fit in here." The belonging begins.

To work most effectively, the leadership of a church must be an endoskeleton (or to use another word, an infrastructure) and not an exoskeleton (or superstructure). Let me explain: When we meet someone on the street, we rarely say, "Wow, nice skeleton." If you see someone's skeleton, they are either suffering from malnutrition or they are no longer alive. Instead, what we see is the soft tissue that covers the skeleton. When people encounter the church, they should encounter the soft tissue of community.

What is this soft tissue?

Real people doing life together.

A sense of belonging.

A family.

Of course, we're not saying that leadership in the church isn't important. An endoskeleton of leadership within the soft tissue is what causes the body to be animated, dynamic, and mobile. If you don't have leadership, you don't have a skeleton, and you end up not with the body of Christ but with a blob of Christ.

Obviously, blobs are not what God intends. Blobs are unable to move on their own, create an infrastructure, or easily align themselves with a common vision. Think of jellyfish and how any movement it makes is gradual and dictated by the tides.

But churches too often function as blobs. A senior leader or key staff member acts as the controlling official, trying to poke and prod at the congregation in an attempt to get them to move in a desired direction or even for any sign of life. Some movement may result from the passionate pulpit messages, but as soon as the poking has stopped, it's all too easy for the blob to return to its original shape. Hence, the church goes from one new church strategy to another trying to get the blob to move.

All this effort with no results generally causes more frustration, and so the leaders try to exert an even greater amount of control. The ultimate result is the exact opposite of what the senior leaders had intended: a continual distancing and decreasing in influence and relevancy between them and congregation (or blob).

Instead of being exoskeletons or blobs, our churches need endoskeletons. An endoskeleton is the power behind the movement and the key component that no one ever sees. It brings structure, intentionality, agility, and life. A jellyfish is at the mercy of the waves, but a fish goes where it wills; the difference is the skeleton.

FOLLOWING THE FLOW

Renewal is vital to leadership. Reforming the skeleton (specifically the endoskeleton) in the church is vital to mobilizing and redirecting the church into its God-given calling and capacity. Now let's return to Ezekiel to find some concluding thoughts around leadership and God's design for the church.

One note before we start: At the beginning of this passage, the man Ezekiel refers to is an angel who had been directing Ezekiel around this prophetic picture of the Temple being rebuilt in Jerusalem. In Ezekiel's day, the Babylonians had destroyed the temple, and the Israelites lived in exile. In this picture, Ezekiel sees a future temple that will one day be rebuilt. Interestingly, this temple was never actually rebuilt. Zerubbabel's temple was rebuilt against both sides of the old temple and was then replaced by Herod's Temple, the one we read about in Jesus' ministry. But Ezekiel received this picture of a future prophetic temple, a House of the Lord.

> [1]Then he brought me back to the door of the temple, and behold, water was issuing from below the threshold of the temple toward the east (for the temple faced east). The water was flowing down from below the south end of the threshold of the temple, south of the altar. [2]Then he brought me out by way of the north gate and led me around on the outside to the outer gate that faces toward the east; and behold, the water was trickling out on the south side.

> [3]Going on eastward with a measuring line in his hand, the man measured a thousand cubits, and then led me through the water, and it was ankle-deep. [4]Again he measured a thousand, and led me through the water, and it was knee-deep. Again he measured a thousand, and led me through the water, and it was waist-deep. [5]Again he measured a thousand, and it was a river that I could not pass through, for the water had risen. It was deep enough to swim in, a river that could not be passed through. [6]And he said to me, "Son of man, have you seen this?"

> Then he led me back to the bank of the river. [7]As I went back, I saw on the bank of the river very many trees on the one side and on the other. [8]And he said to me, "This water flows toward the eastern region and goes down into the Arabah, and enters the sea; when the water flows into the sea, the water will become fresh. [9]And wherever the river goes, every living creature that swarms will live, and there will be very many fish. For this water goes there, that the waters of the sea may become fresh; so everything will live where the river goes. [10]Fishermen will stand beside the sea. From Engedi to Eneglaim it will be a place for the spreading of nets. Its fish will be of very many kinds, like the fish of the Great Sea. [11]But its swamps and marshes will not become fresh; they are to be left for salt. [12]And on the banks, on both sides of the river, there will grow all kinds of

trees for food. Their leaves will not wither, nor their fruit fail, but they will bear fresh fruit every month, because the water for them flows from the sanctuary. Their fruit will be for food, and their leaves for healing."[46]

In this passage, the temple is rebuilt and reformed, incidentally in precisely the same order in which the army is reformed from dry bones. Both receive new life from the first task of reforming. Ezekiel 47 says that the temple must be rebuilt before the water can flow, just as Ezekiel 37 indicates that the bones have to be drawn together and covered with flesh and muscle before they can receive the breath of God. In this passage, Ezekiel first saw the temple reforming, and then out of the reformation, renewal begins to bubble up out of the Holy Place. Renewal comes out of the place where people meet with God in worship, in the place of engaging God face to face.

Out of this place, a spring bubbles up. First, a little stream flows out from the temple, through its doors, down its steps, and past the south side of the altar. Then the stream turns left and flows out of the south gate. From there, it takes a hard left and flows east. This is important imagery both to Ezekiel and to the Israelites who heard his prophecy. Here's why: Pilgrims always entered the temple courts through the north gate and left through the south gate.

That means this stream flows in the direction of the people *leaving* worship.

Where does God's life go after it bubbles up in worship? It always goes out. **The Spirit that we engage with in worship, that we receive and encounter as the people of God, will always lead us in the direction of our mission with God.** It will *always* lead us out. If you go out by another gate, you will miss the river and miss the Spirit.

The imagery goes even further.

Remember that after the river flows out of the south side, it turns toward the east. At this point, the Israelites

THE SPIRIT that we engage with in worship, that we receive and encounter as the people of God, will always lead us in the direction of our mission with God.

---

[46] Ezekiel 47

hearing this prophecy would have gasped. For them, going east meant going toward the enemies of God. Going east meant going toward Edom and so many other nations that had set themselves up against God. It meant going toward the Dead Sea, a visible sign of God's judgment, because it was where Sodom and Gomorrah were covered in the salty ash of God's judgment.

The river flows eastward across the Judean Uplands, continually getting deeper and deeper. The first measuring point indicates that the river is ankle-deep. This was deep enough for all of those liturgical Christians, because it was deep enough to baptize children in. Then, the angel measures off another distance, and the river is knee-deep. If you've been in a river that's knee-deep and moving, you know that you have to watch your footing because you can easily lose your balance. It's almost as though the river wants to pick you up.

The angel measures off another distance, and the water is up to the waist. In a fast-moving river at this depth, you would really be struggling to stand and move. Then, the angel measures off another distance, and the river is too deep to cross on your feet. You now have to swim. Depending on the speed of the water, the river will take you where it will. But it is at this point that the river is surrounded by trees on both banks.

Then, the angel leads Ezekiel back to the bank of the river. To Ezekiel's surprise, trees were growing on both sides of the river. "All kinds of fruit trees will grow along both sides of the river. The leaves of these trees will never turn brown and fall, and there will always be fruit on their branches. There will be a new crop every month, without fail! For they are watered by the river flowing from the Temple. The fruit will be for food and the leaves for healing."[47]

The trees flourish only when the water is too deep to stand in and the river is fully flowing. Supernatural provision and the power for healing and growth occur only when our feet are off the ground. When we can no longer control the direction that we're going in, we have to surrender to the direction of the river, and that supernatural, continuous provision comes to us from the Holy Spirit comes to us.

The river flows east through the desert into the Jordan Valley and then enters

....

[47] Ezekiel 47:12

the Dead Sea. The waters of this stream will heal the salty waters of the Dead Sea and make them fresh and pure. Then it goes down into the Arabar.

It goes down?

Yes, it goes down 1,300 feet below sea level. This river flows down from the Judean uplands, down the escarpment of the Rift Valley in which the Jordan River flows and then toward the Dead Sea. That rift valley is the face of the largest waterfall on planet Earth. Four times the height of Niagara Falls, twice as high as Victoria Falls. This is a wonder of the world that goes down topographically and geographically to the lowest place on the face of the Earth.

The life of God's spirit encountered in worship is looking for the lowest place, the deadliest place, so it can bring life there. So following the river means going to certain death. Is it any wonder many will get out of the river before they go over the edge?

The *Arabar* means "the great depression" in Hebrew. It's a fitting name, because it is a place where you find only death because it's so low and so salty that nothing lives there. But when the river flows there, it turns everything into what appears to be a Garden of Eden. Everything begins to live. There are fish in the Dead Sea like the fish of the Great Sea. There are many places for spreading nets.

A STORY FROM ARABAR

I have seen this kind of thing happen. Today, St. Thomas is now two churches, St. Thomas Philadelphia and St. Thomas Crookes, and life is springing up everywhere. They now have over 300 mid-size communities, and those mid-size communities are all functioning as missional communities in the hardest and most difficult communities that you can imagine. They are seeing a harvest, catching fish as they spread the nets of grace and love.

About a decade ago, I preached this message on Ezekiel at an Anglican church in Pawleys Island, South Carolina, called All Saints Episcopal Church. This message is generally the first thing I look to preach whenever I'm invited to speak somewhere, because it was the very first sermon I preached at St. Thomas. It became the underlying theological theme for us as a community.

We were following in the river until the river took us to the Arabar.

Eventually, what following the river meant was this: Because disciples are very good at finding fish, we grew rapidly. The building was overflowing. We had four services on Sunday, and we couldn't fit any more. We needed space. So I went to see the Bishop. I said: "Bishop, we've been trying this thing called discipleship."

He said, "That sounds very interesting."

I said to him, "I'd like you, if you would, to give us some of the old buildings that are redundant around here in Sheffield, like they did in London with Holy Trinity Brompton."

He replied: "Over my dead body." (This may be a paraphrase.)

I said, "OK, what would you like me to do then?"

He pondered this for a few minutes and finally said: "I'd like you to stop growing. Just contain what is going on in your church and do the job of a parish priest."

I went back to my church certain that this wasn't a word from the Lord. I knew that I wasn't going to take on the spiritual authorities of the church; rather, I needed to find a way around them. At the time, it was a big deal in England to move your people outside of your geographical parish. You're only allowed to minister in a certain area, and sadly most bishops are more interested in control and order than seeing new people come into the Kingdom.

So we were growing, we had no room, and the area bishop was unwilling to help. After weeks of praying and searching for a larger place, we found a large gymnasium downtown. I quietly inquired with a few pastors as to which parish the building was in, and I discovered it was in the cathedral's parish. I wrote the bishop outlining our plan and asked if I could discuss it with him.

Thankfully, he agreed to discuss it.

But when I arrived at the bishop's office for our conversation, I found the bishop, the assistant bishop, two archdeacons, and the dean of the cathedral. It was clear the intention was intimidation. They asked question after question and basically told me that if I did this, it would be rebellion.

So what was I to do? I felt a bit like Peter in front of the Sanhedrin. Should I obey men, or the sense that I heard God speak to me? I decided speaking this question out loud would appear to be too arrogant of a statement, especially to the ears of the Anglican elite in front of me. In that moment God gave me an idea. I asked the bishop if he would allow me to use the gymnasium as an "experiment." Generally, an experiment means a good idea in England. Over the years, I've moved organs, chairs, rearranged rooms — all for experimental periods of time. (Note that most of these "experiments" are still ongoing.)

At this point, the group knew I wasn't going to back down, and so the experimental option was a great path forward. Everyone agreed. And that was the beginning of all the Missional Communities that would come out of that one decision.

Fast forward a few years, and interestingly, the Queen of England signed an order the day I got on a plane to fly to the United States that said this experiment was no longer an experiment, but instead, the very first example of the new order of churches where Christians could function in other people's parishes. She signed it with her own signature on her desk the day I left.
I can tell you this: Those 10 years were really tough, but today the river is in the Arabar.

If you were a prostitute in Sheffield, it used to be really difficult to find Jesus because there was no way into the body of Christ. If you were poor and from generations of lostness, it was very difficult to become a Christian. If you were an ordinary person who struggled with the burdens of life, it was very hard to find anybody who would listen to you, pray for you on the streets, and bring you a touch of healing.

Today it's much easier. In the last 6 months alone, more than 700 people who had never darkened the door of the church became Christians because the church followed the river into the Arabar. The crime rate is dropping.

The Arabar is coming alive, and there are many places for spreading nets for the harvest of fish.

Why? The reason is that the church took the redirection, however shocking it was, and followed the river eastward toward the great waterfall that meant certain death if we went over it, landing into in great depression. There they discovered that not only was their life preserved, but life came to others as well. And so in the Arabar of Sheffield, the process of renewal begins over and over again.

WHAT'S YOUR STORY?

Now imagine that we fast-forward 10 years into the future.

Rather than changing our understanding of what it means to be the church and embracing our missional calling of making disciples and seeing the Kingdom come to earth, we played it safe. We embraced what we quickly saw as a precipitous and inevitable decline. If we do that, the Arabar will come to America. Even now, we are already seeing it.
We will have missed the Millenial Generation, which is already larger than the entire Boomer population, previously the largest generation in history. Imagine a world where only 4 percent of Boomers were Christians. America would look *identical* to the way Europe is today because that's exactly what happened with Europe. A generation went missing.

Today, in the United States, you will only find 4 percent of Millenials in a church service on any given Sunday. They are quickly becoming the missing generation.

But with the leading of the Holy Spirit and a re-imagining of what it means to be a disciple and a missional leader, it doesn't have to be this way.

You see, the story of thousands and thousands who are in Sheffield, the United States, and now across the world can be your story. This is the kind of mission that you are called to lead. You're called to lead a reformation that comes from reforming the body. You're called to redirect that body toward the purposes that Christ has for it. You're called to lead people to seek God and his renewing touch, so that they may have the vitality and life to do the thing that we've been called to do.

But you can only do this if you're a missional leader who is multiplying missional leaders. To make this kind of difference, you will need to recruit leaders with character and competency, and disciple them through the leadership pipeline with continual training, deployment, and review, slowly forming you into a leadership household... a family. You will need to find leaders from all five of the fivefold ministries and help them grow not only in their base ministry but also in phases of the other four as well. You will have to work together to properly align covenant and capitals, and you will have to develop a common vocab that guides you together to the mission God is calling you to fulfill. We want, we need, leaders like this to be multiplied in our midst over and over again.

Reformation and renewal can happen in and around you like it has in Arabar and Sheffield and other places across the world and across the ages. As we said in the introduction, **this is meant to be your story as well — a story of shaping and multiplying missional leaders who can lead the people of God to their destiny**. Let us join Jesus, Paul, and so many others in multiplying missional leaders, and let us pray for God to bring renewal and reformation and a great harvest in our stories as well.

IF YOU ENJOYED THIS BOOK,
HERE ARE TWO OTHERS YOU'LL WANT TO READ,
AVAILABLE IN PAPERBACK AND EBOOK:

Building a Discipling Culture

There is a discipleship crisis in the Western church. Many Christians may come to a worship service, join a small group or even tithe, but few have the kind of transformed lives we read about in Scripture. If we made disciples like Jesus made them, we wouldn't have a problem finding leaders or seeing new people come to faith. Building a Discipling Culture is the product of 25+ years of hands-on discipleship practice — developed in a post-Christian context, tackling how to make the types of missional disciples Jesus spoke of.

Launching Missional Communities: A Field Guide

Among church practitioners, "Missional Communities" have become one of the most discussed tools of the past 20 years. This is a book about where they came from, how they developed and how your community can begin launching and multiplying them to see those who don't know Jesus begin the journey of discipleship. It is a practical, insider's look, giving you the tools to make MCs come alive in your church.

You can find additional resources by Mike Breen and the 3DM team at
www.weare3DM.com

Follow us online:
Blog: mikebreen.wordpress.com • Twitter: @mike_breen • Facebook: /WeAre3DM